A LITTLE HISTORY
OF ANTIQUES

For Vanessa

A LITTLE HISTORY OF ANTIQUES

Nicholas Courtney

MICHAEL JOSEPH
LONDON

MICHAEL JOSEPH LTD

Published by the Penguin Group
27 Wrights Lane, London W8 5TZ
Viking Penguin Inc., 375 Hudson Street, New York, New York 10014, USA
Penguin Books Australia Ltd, Ringwood, Victoria, Australia
Penguin Books Canada Ltd, 10 Alcorn Avenue, Toronto, Ontario, Canada M4V 3B2
Penguin Books (NZ) Ltd, 182–190 Wairau Road, Auckland 10, New Zealand

Penguin Books Ltd, Registered Offices: Harmondsworth, Middlesex, England

First published in Great Britain 1994

Typeset in Trump Medieval 9/10½ point

Design and computer page make-up by
Tony & Penny Mills

Printed in Great Britain by
Butler & Tanner Ltd,
Frome and London

A CIP catalogue record for this book is available
from the British Library

ISBN 0 7181 3659 4

CONTENTS

INTRODUCTION

This is an age of ever-increasing interest in antiques and the past which made them. Our interest is fostered by the many historic houses open to the public, by new, enlivened museums, and by television programmes celebrating our heritage. Yet however much we admire antiques for their decorative value (rather than merely their monetary value), they remain isolated, meaningless objects unless we understand their context. A little knowledge of how they were made and of their materials, of who crafted and designed them, and of their subsequent use, gives a new dimension to every piece. To appreciate fully each antique, and to understand how it fitted into the world for which it was made, is to bring it to life. Such knowledge enhances not only ownership but also any visit to an historic house, museum, antique shop or auction room.

The subject of antiques is immensely wide; the scope is as large as it is fascinating. Invariably, there is some little-known 'nugget' of information to make even the most ordinary piece intriguing. The aim of this book is to present those nuggets succinctly, so that the reader responds, 'How interesting, I didn't know that!'

DATING THE ENGLISH PERIODS DESCRIBED IN THE TEXT

The **Middle Ages** is an ill-defined period of about a thousand years that spans the downfall of the ancient civilizations of Greece and Rome and the dawn of the Renaissance in Europe. Roughly, it dates from the 5th century to the mid-15th century (1453, the Fall of Constantinople). The **Dark Ages** applies to the early centuries of the Middle Ages, **Saxon** and **Norman** cover the 10th, 11th and 12th centuries, and **medieval** applies to the 13th and 14th centuries.

The **Tudor** period (1485–1603) includes the reigns of Henry VII, Henry VIII, Edward VI, Mary I and Elizabeth I. The last Tudor monarch is also accorded a period of her own, **Elizabethan** (or late Tudor), which spans the second half of the 16th century.

Most of the 17th century falls into the **Stuart** period, which is divided into the reigns of the monarchs: **Jacobean** (James I, 1603–25), **Carolean** (Charles I, 1625–49), **Commonwealth**, **Puritan** or **Cromwellian** (the Interregnum period, 1649–60), and **Restoration** (Charles I and James II, 1660–89). Sometimes these periods are simplified into early and late Stuart. **William and Mary** and William III (1689–1702) are virtually the same styles, while **Queen Anne** (1702–14) is a style on its own. She is the only monarch whose period is given her proper, full title.

With the House of Hanover came the **Early Georgian** period (George I and George II, 1714–60) and **Georgian** (1760–85), much of the reign of George III. The **Regency** period begins in about 1785, well before the Prince of Wales actually became Regent in 1811, and includes his reign as George IV and that of his brother, William IV, who died in 1837. This is followed by the **Victorian** age (Victoria 1837–1901), for most of the rest of the 19th century, although the term **Edwardian** pre-dates the death of Queen Victoria in 1901.

THE STYLES

Throughout Europe, the two styles associated with the Middle Ages are **Romanesque** and **Gothic.** The former, as its name implies, is based on Roman methods of building (the round arch) and was born out of a time of revival of empires and invasions past; it dates roughly between AD 600 and 1150. In England between the mid-10th and 12th centuries, it was termed **Norman**. Although Gothic drew on the Romanesque style, it was in many ways a reaction to it. Evolving in an era of castles, crusades and chivalry, it was prevalent throughout Europe between the 12th and 16th centuries. It was characterized by the pointed arch. The style was thought to be Islamic in origin, brought to Spain by the Moors in the 9th century and spreading throughout the rest of Europe from the 12th century. The name was coined by Renaissance architects who considered the pointed Gothic arch 'barbarian', like the Goths who rampaged through Europe between the 3rd and 5th centuries. Apart from an abundance of architecture, genuine articles from this period are far from common.

The artistic period known as the **Renaissance** (literally 'rebirth') originated in Italy, where the wealth of classical remains and the new excavations in and around Rome led to a reappraisal of the classical traditions of form and ornament. As Italian wealth was paramount throughout Europe, and as Greece was occupied by a Muslim colonial power, it was inevitable that the origins of a cultural rejuvenation in the 15th century should stem from there. The Renaissance had been established in Italy for about a hundred years before its full impact was felt elsewhere in Europe. The Early Renaissance dates from about 1420 to 1500, the High Renaissance from 1500 to about 1540, the period loosely corresponding with the early Tudor in England. While this new age was dawning in the rest of Europe, a new interpretation of classicism, that also incorporated motifs of Islamic origin, was evolving in Italy. This is now known as **mannerism**, and dates from about 1540 to 1580. The style which began with Michelangelo, afforded an intellectual stimulus and a free expression, where classical theories were stretched to heighten dramatic effect and emotion. In England, there is more evidence of this movement in furniture than in architecture.

Corresponding in time with the early and late Stuart periods is the **baroque** style which swept Europe during the 17th century, although it was not seen in England until the second decade, and lasted until the 1720s. The name baroque comes from the Portuguese *barroco*, meaning a rough or imperfect shell, a pejorative term coined by later classical purists

*A painted armchair
after an Italian
model, c.1625*

to describe the style's unclassical use of the classical
form. Giovanni Lorenzo Bernini (1598–1680) is
credited as the instigator of the baroque style, and it
spread through Europe due to the power of the papacy
and the influence of Louis XIV in France. It is a style
of grandeur, the ultimate embodiment of princely
state. In England the period from about 1680 to 1715
was characterized by **Palladianism**, a return to a severe
form of classicism as interpreted by the Italian
architect Andrea Palladio (1518–80). This set the
standard for the neo-classical style of the late 18th
century.

Before this, however, came the **rococo** style. It
originated in Italy, developed in France at the court of
Louis XV and arrived in England in the 1730s to be
interpreted in an English manner. It is characterized
by extreme freedom and the graceful use of flowing
curves ('C' and 'S' scrolls). Its form combined
asymmetrical and elaborate ornament, even frivolity,
frequently mixed with elements of naturalism.
Predominant themes were flowers and anything to do
with water, notably shells, water nymphs and Nereids,
and stylized rocks, hence the name rococo from the
French *rocaille*, a rock. Like baroque, the term rococo

was used pejoratively by later designers for anything overblown and shallow.

A style associated with rococo (but not part of it) in the mid-18th century was **chinoiserie**, the English designers' recurring interpretation of the Chinese taste for the exotic. Equally whimsical was the beginning of the **Gothic revival.** In the 1750s an interest was revived in romantic medieval forms, and this Gothic revival was considered more patriotic than the adoption of the Chinese or Oriental style. The house built by the art collector and patron Horace Walpole at Strawberry Hill, Twickenham was a showpiece for this style. This early Gothic revival lasted only a few years, but the style was to return to fashion in the early 19th century.

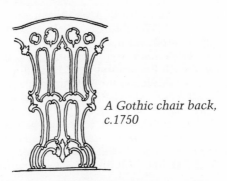

A Gothic chair back, c.1750

The fundamental classicism of the Renaissance endured until the 18th century, albeit greatly modified by baroque and rococo. Although in some ways a reaction against the flowery, sometimes frivolous rococo, the **neo-classical** style that was introduced to England by Robert Adam (qv) in 1765 was therefore not new, but a different interpretation of the classical original. The origins of this neo-classicism lay not in metropolitan Rome but in the newly discovered Roman towns of Pompeii, Herculaneum and Paestum, which yielded more examples of classical architecture and decoration. The style attempted to reproduce the simplicity and grandeur of classical forms, which were seen as embodying reason and order. Towards the end of the 18th century a **Greek revival**, fostered by such works as *Antiquities of Athens* by James 'Athenian' Stuart, became fashionable. Furniture designs and motifs for decoration were taken directly from Greek painted vases, sometimes, as in chair design, successfully, in other cases less so. The revival, in part, led to the next style, the Regency.

The *Directoire* style in France that followed the French Revolution of 1789 was a severe interpretation of classical forms – plain mahogany, straight lines with gilt-bronze classical mounts. Towards the end of the 18th century the new wealth and stability of the monied classes under Napoleon Bonaparte, first as Consul, then as Emperor, prompted a more opulent style of furnishing now known as the French Empire style. Again, the theme was classical, the motifs copied from vases. After Napoleon's campaign in Egypt in 1789, sphinxes, scarabs and zoomorphic gods (represented as animals), were further embellishments.

The **Regency** style is so strongly associated with the French Empire style that it is often called 'English Empire'. Although the Regency of the Prince of Wales lasted from 1811 to 1820, the style actually spanned more than 50 years, from about 1785 to the accession of Queen Victoria. It began as an extension of the Greek revival, with copies of designs and motifs from vases, and the no-nonsense *Directoire* style with its clean-cut lines. Motifs were also 'anglicized', such as

An armchair from Hope's Household Furniture, *1807*

the lion's mask and hairy paw, or ram's head. Nelson's sea victories prompted a range of nautical additions like ropes and anchors. As in France, the Egyptian theme was strong, with the winged sphinx and papyrus leaves. Slowly, the simplicity was eroded and the style became more lavish.

At the end of the 18th century and the beginning of the 19th, it was firmly held that there would soon be a new monarch, and with the new reign would come a new style. Consequently during this period (which also coincided with the Napoleonic Wars when too French a taste might be considered unpatriotic), there was a constant change in style. The Prince of Wales revived chinoiserie for his Brighton Pavilion and the drawing room at Carlton House. The Gothic revival too became popular in the wake of romantic literature.

The taste, rather than style, of the long **Victorian** age is often described as eclectic. Much of it, however, was influenced more by such considerations as ease of machine manufacture than by underlying stylistic developments. It borrowed from, and built on, four main styles – the Greek revival, Elizabethan, what can very loosely be described as Louis XIV and, most of all, the Gothic revival. Once again the Gothic revival became the national style, which was extensively used

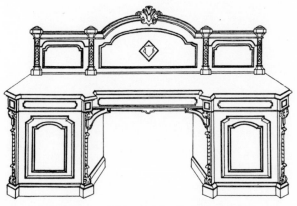

A Victorian sideboard in the Elizabethan style, c.1845

for grand, public buildings, not least for the rebuilding of the Houses of Parliament after their destruction by fire in 1835. In addition to those four main styles, the revivals of chinoiserie (japanning qv) and rococo, and later the Japanese influence, made for rather a confused array of styles. As a direct reaction against this miscellany and machine-made, mass-produced articles, came the **Arts and Crafts** movement, a revival of interest in the craftsmanship of the Middle Ages, which lasted from 1880 to the First World War.

FURNITURE

INTRODUCTION

Furniture (in French *meubles* and in German *Möbel*) is, by definition, a collection of 'movable articles in a dwelling house', as opposed to fixtures and fittings, which are not portable. The term originated in the Middle Ages when nobles moved between their houses with their furniture piled on to baggage carts and consequently the majority of early furniture was made for the upper classes whose lifestyle demanded easily transportable furniture. By contrast, the houses of the lower orders were virtually bare.

Other than chests, few examples of furniture from before the Tudor period have survived. The re-invention of the saw-pit in England in the 15th century meant that logs could be sawn into planks (as opposed to being split into uneven thicknesses). This led to a system whereby a rectangular frame could be filled with loose panels, as in a large settle (qv) or the sides of a chest. Panelling also overcame the problem of wood shrinking, warping or splitting.

Surviving furniture of the Tudor period is mostly of oak, an indigenous tree to England, although there are references to pieces in walnut that were carved and painted or gilded. Much Dutch furniture was imported through Antwerp, and this introduced the current styles of the Low Countries, such as the bulbous table legs and bed-posts so characteristic of the Elizabethan period.

The innovative elements of European design were lacking in the English furniture of the early 17th century, the Jacobean and Carolean periods. Oak furniture was plain or carved in low relief, with applied split turnings as the usual adornment. Fine furniture was 'not merchantable' during the Civil War and the Commonwealth. With the Restoration, English furniture makers advanced from their 'vulgar and pitiful' beginnings to master a high standard of joinery, cabinet making and locksmithing, along with the skills of marquetry (qv). With the new order came a more complex form of society that required more sophisticated furniture – bookcases, writing desks, chests of drawers, better lighting and mirrors. Walnut replaced oak for this refined furniture, and the trend for finer furniture continued throughout the reigns of William and Mary, with strong Dutch and French influences, and Queen Anne, where the fashion for carving was replaced by a simpler line and a walnut veneer.

The furniture of the Georgian period is characterized by the phasing out of walnut as the preferred wood and the introduction, after 1733, of mahogany. Throughout the rest of the 18th century a vast proliferation of furniture was made for every conceivable use. Until then all fine furniture had been made either for the Crown or for the houses of the rich land-owning classes. The burgeoning middle class, with money to spend on furnishing their houses, provided a ready market for furniture makers.

With the exploration and colonization of the Americas and the Far East came a wealth of new woods. These in turn gave rise to new styles of furniture, as with satinwood (qv) towards the end of the 18th century. Satinwood was principally used for drawing room furniture, while mahogany remained the preferred wood for the dining room and library. Rosewood (qv) suited the plainer styles of the Regency.

With the advent of the industrialization during the Victorian period came the mechanization of much of the furniture maker's craft. Once again furniture became heavy and ornate, often deeply carved when following an earlier style. New media, such as papier mâché (qv), were introduced. Mass production meant cheaper pieces, and thus furniture became affordable to far greater numbers of people – a far cry from the bare houses of the medieval peasant.

THE CRAFT

Early medieval furniture was the work of the carpenter, who pieced together solid planks of wood, usually oak, with a series of pegs, known as 'tre' nails, and wedges. By the early 16th century, the **mortise and tenon** joint was in use in England. This basic technique of joining two pieces of timber, where the shaped end of one piece, the tenon, fits exactly into a rectangular hole in another, the mortise, had been used by the ancient Egyptians. The joint was held by a wooden peg, or dowel. The craftsman was called a 'joyner' or **joiner**. His tools were saws, planes, chisels and an adze, a cutting tool resembling a pick with the blade at right angles to the shaft.

A mortise and tenon joint

Another skill perfected by the ancient Egyptians that came to England with the Romans was the art of turning, to shape a piece of wood, such as a chair leg, in the round. The **turner** used a simple pole lathe, where a cord was attached at one end to a springy pole (often a living sapling in the forest), and at the other to a treadle, with the middle wound around the piece to be turned. This primitive, but effective, method survived in some rural areas until the 19th century.

Several important developments in furniture making occurred in the last quarter of the 17th century, when new skills and techniques came to England from France and the Low Countries at the Restoration. Two of these were the invention of the more sophisticated **dovetail** joint, and of better, stronger glues. The dovetail is a superior mortise and tenon joint, triangular in shape like a dove's tail, rather than rectangular, and therefore far stronger. The new, stronger glues obviated the need for a joining dowel. This allowed furniture to be lighter and more refined, particularly in the drawers. In better quality furniture the drawer linings (the sides and bottom boards) were made of oak to withstand the constant wear and friction, whereas in country pieces they were generally of pine, which was less hardwearing. One method of dating a piece of furniture is to examine the direction of the grain of the bottom boards of the drawers – in those made before 1730 the grain runs lengthways, after that date it runs crossways.

A dovetail joint

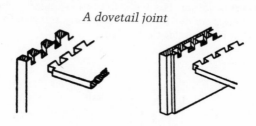

Handmade nails were used by all furniture makers until the late 17th century. The earliest screws were introduced in about 1675 and were also handmade. The thread was filed by hand and had no point. Later screws were turned on a lathe. An unlikely screw-turner was Louis XVI of France.

With this better made furniture came the craft of the **cabinet maker**, whose expertise exceeded those of a mere joiner, both in the construction of the carcase, and in its decoration. Techniques for decorating pieces of furniture became increasingly sophisticated as the cabinet maker's skill advanced.

Inlay is a technique where pieces of different coloured woods of anything up to ¼ inch thick are set individually into a piece of furniture to make either a geometric or a floral design. The art was practised by the ancient Egyptians, and was revived in England in the 16th century. Ebony (qv) or bog oak (qv) was used for black, holly for white, and yew, sycamore (which took a stain well) and fruit woods for other colours.

Bone, ivory and mother-of-pearl were also common inlays. Richly decorated chests from the 16th and early 17th centuries are often called Nonsuch Chests, after one piece which depicts in inlay Henry VIIIth's Nonsuch Palace in Ewell in Surrey. Thin strips of boxwood or ebony were commonly inlaid around the exposed edges of furniture, particularly drawers, because, being extremely hard, they helped to protect the edges from damage.

Marquetry differs from inlay in that the design is made up separately from various coloured woods, and then applied as a separate panel to the piece of furniture. Sheets of different coloured wood veneers are bonded together and the design cut out with a fret-saw. The design is then reassembled using different backgrounds and cutouts to make up coloured patterns. The discarded backgrounds and pieces were reused in another form. Often the cutouts were scorched to give a shaded effect.

Marquetry

A similar technique was perfected by a Frenchman, André Charles **Boulle** (1642–1732), *ébéniste* (furniture maker) to Louis XIV, who used sheets of brass and tortoiseshell (occasionally silver and ivory as well) for his marquetry panels. The sheets were placed together and the design cut out; the two panels were then separated, the detail of one being put into the other. Where the tortoiseshell predominates the effect is called *première partie*, where the brass predominates, it is *contre partie*. Boulle furniture was made in England after 1810, principally by William Holmes

Baldock. While marquetry is used to create naturalistic designs, such as flowers and birds, with **parquetry** the resulting design is geometric, as on a parquet floor.

In the mid-17th century the spa-town of Tunbridge Wells in Kent became famous for its **Tunbridgeware**, a form of inlay work where thousands of minute strips of wood in natural colours are up-ended and glued together to form a mosaic design when viewed from above. The whole block is then cut into slices, like a veneer, and applied to a wide variety of wooden objects such as trays and boxes, napkin rings and cribbage boards. Cheaper copies produced in the late 19th century ruined the Tunbridge craftsmen's trade.

Veneering is the disguising of a common wood with a thin layer of a more exotic timber, attached with glue. The ancient Egyptians were skilled in the art of veneering, the Romans too – Pliny the Elder recommended it in AD 77 – but the art was lost during the Dark Ages after the fall of Rome in the 5th century. It was rediscovered by the French in the early 17th century. In England it was widely practised in the 17th, 18th and 19th centuries, initially as a means of conserving stocks of walnut, then for utilizing rare and expressive woods imported from abroad that were too expensive to use in their solid form. Sheets of veneer were cut by hand in varying thicknesses, from $\frac{1}{16}$ inch to as much as $\frac{1}{8}$ for walnut. Today, modern technology can produce a veneer sheet $\frac{1}{64}$ inch thick. The most interesting veneers are cut from near a branch on the trunk, or from a root malformation, to give varied patterns and textures such as 'oyster-shells', 'burr' or 'pollard'. Even quite ordinary timbers could be used for veneering, provided they had an interesting defect – walnut, pollarded oak, elm, ash and yew, as well as maple for its distinctive 'bird's-eye' effect. Strips of veneer were often used as further decoration, principally around the edges of the piece. These narrow strips have the grain running either straight across, where it is called 'cross-banding', or diagonally, called 'feathering'. 'Herringbone' is where two feathered strips are mounted at 90 degrees.

Another craft connected with the cabinet maker from the 17th century onwards was the **staining** and polishing of furniture. The purpose of staining was either to enhance the look of the wood's natural grain, or to make an ordinary wood more exciting. Pine and pearwood were stained black, or ebonized, to resemble ebony; beech could be stained to look like either walnut or mahogany. When sycamore was given a greyish-green hue it was known as **harewood**. In the 18th century (when it was known as air-wood) sycamore was stained with a liquid made from rusty nails and vinegar. Other stains were made from natural sources, such as roots and berries, and oxides.

Most furniture was finished by **polishing**, which not only sealed the wood but also enhanced the grain and figuring. **Patina** is the result of years of general use, wear and tear, sunlight and, in particular, dust falling on this repeatedly polished surface. The result is a deep, rich shine. From the 16th century onwards beeswax, either in its solid state or dissolved in turpentine (a distillation of resin from conifers), was rubbed into the wood, then buffed up with a cloth or brush. Vegetable oils and resins were an alternative. Powdered brick dust was sometimes used for filling the grain and absorbing the beeswax.

Sheraton's (qv) recipe for a polishing wax taken from his *Cabinet Dictionary* of 1803 was to ' . . . take bees wax and a small quantity of turpentine in a clean earthen pan, and set it over the fire till the wax unites with the turpentine, which it will do by constant stirring about: add to this a little red lead finely ground upon a stone, together with a small portion of fine Oxford oachre, to bring the whole to the colour of brisk mahogany. Lastly, when you take it off the fire, add a little copal varnish to it, and mix it well together, then turn the whole into a bason of water, and while it is yet warm, work it into a ball, with which the brush is to be rubbed as before observed. And observe, with a ball of wax and brush kept for this purpose entirely, furniture in general may be kept in good order.'

French polish was developed in France in the early 18th century but it was not known in England before

1815. Its main ingredient, shellac, is the resinous secretion of an insect, the *Coccus lacca*, (named after the Hindi word *lakh*, meaning gum). The shellac is dissolved in a spirit, usually methylated spirit, and worked into the wooden surface with a cloth. The wood is then polished with a little linseed and finished off with more shellac mixed with spirit. The process survives little changed today.

True **lacquer-work** was first made in China in the 4th millennium BC, but the craft did not reach Europe until the 16th century. Lacquer is made from the resin tapped from the lacquer-tree (*Rhus vernicifera*), to which coloured pigments are added. The mixture is then applied to wood and allowed to dry. The surface is rubbed down with pumice, another coat is applied and the process repeated at least 20 times. There can be as many as 200 coats on a piece that has to be deeply carved. The result is a highly polished, incredibly hard surface. To ensure that there was no dust and that the lacquer dried slowly, the walls of the workshop ran with water (the workers did not last long in such an unhealthy climate), or the piece would be taken out to sea. Lacquer-work became fashionable in England after the Restoration when Charles II returned from exile in France with acquired French and Dutch taste, and particularly through his Portuguese wife, Catherine of Braganza, who brought the Portuguese trading concession in the Far East as her dowry.

It was not possible, however, for Europeans to work in real lacquer. Even when the exact tree that yielded the lacquer resin was discovered by European naturalists in 1720, it could not successfully be grown in the West. As the resin could not be transported from the Far East without drying solid, Europeans had to make their own imitation lacquer, applied by a process called **japanning**. The craft was first developed towards the end of the 17th century, and was stimulated after the publication in 1688 of Stalker and Parker's *Treatise of Japanning and Varnishing*. It gave detailed recipes for making different varnishes, the choice of metals (mostly brass-dust that resembled gold, silver dust, and powdered tin) used in decoration, the colours (usually black but also red, green, yellow and brown), and cutout patterns for decoration. The process of japanning entailed dissolving shellac in a 'spirit of wine' (alcohol) with a pigment which was then painted on to the piece of furniture in thin coats to simulate real lacquer. As with the Oriental lacquering, the process of painting and smoothing was repeated many times. Stalker and Parker also owned a shop in London selling all the materials to cater for the more artistic wanting to decorate their own furniture and boxes. Many of these genteel amateur lacquerists showed great skill.

Gesso furniture reached its height of popularity in the early 18th century, but declined soon after. Here the piece of furniture is roughly carved, then covered with between ten and 20 layers of gesso, a mixture of chalk and parchment-chippings size. The hardened gesso can then be carved and the piece gilded with either gold or silver leaf, applied with rabbit's-skin glue. A half-ounce gold ingot, when beaten out, could cover a football pitch. As gold does not tarnish, it was more widely used than silver.

Papier mâché came to England from France in the 1670s, but was little used until the mid-18th century when it became a popular medium for furniture and decorative work. It is created by an ingenious process whereby paper is either pulped and mixed with chalk and glue before being pressed into a mould, or built up in layers with flour and water paste. In the 18th century, papier mâché was chiefly used as a substitute for plaster in cornices and wall decoration. The process was later expanded to the widespread manufacture of all types of furniture, from the smallest box, chair or table to cabinets and double beds in the Victorian era. Oval trays are the most common survivors today.

THE MATERIALS

The types of wood used for furniture have always been governed by both availability and fashion. Trees fall into two categories: hardwoods, as a rule deciduous, broad-leaved trees; and softwoods, usually evergreen and coniferous, such as all the pines. Most fine antique furniture was made from hardwoods such as oak, mahogany or walnut, while cheaper, country pieces or carcases were constructed from pine.

Trees used for making furniture were felled and the branches removed. The trunk was then put in a river, secured by a chain through a hole in the top, and left to soak for at least a year. It was then left to dry for a further two years before being planked. The planks were left to season, one year for every inch of thickness. With such a lengthy process, the furniture maker was assuring his own, and his successor's, future supply.

From Tudor times onwards travelling sawyers moved from estate to estate planking timber with their long, two-handled saws. The senior man would stand at the top of the saw pit guiding the saw, while the junior below pulled the blade downwards. Not only did he do all the hard work, he also had the added discomfort of the sawdust falling in his face. Saw pits were superseded by the circular saw in about 1790, and the band saw came into use from about 1858. Thus a piece of furniture with circular saw marks is unlikely to pre-date 1790.

Oak. As an indigenous tree, oak was most commonly used for all English furniture until the end of the 17th century, when it became less fashionable. The wood's close grain makes it less susceptible to rot and woodworm than other timbers such as ash, chestnut, sycamore, elm and beech, which is why so much early oak furniture has survived. **Bog oak**, as its name implies, is oak that has lain for centuries in a bog – usually an Irish bog. Consequently it is dense, and so extremely hardwearing. The best quality oak, called 'wainscot oak', comes from the two boards cut from the centre of the trunk, and only this wood was used for furniture making. Imported oak from Russia,

Germany, Poland and Holland was also known as **wainscot oak**. The term 'wainscot' was later used for the panelling of a room, regardless of the type of the timber used. When plasterwork wall decoration came into fashion in the late 17th century, the wainscot became narrower. Where it was dispensed with altogether, the iron hoops of the ladies' skirts damaged the plaster at floor level. A single plank, later known as a **skirting board**, was fixed around the room to protect the walls.

Walnut. The walnut tree was probably introduced to Britain by the Romans. It became widely used for fine furniture in the 17th century, initially solid, and later as a veneer. Walnut was also imported from France. So popular was it that the period between the Restoration and the reign of George I (1660–1714) is often known as 'the age of walnut'. After the Great Fire of London in 1666, houses were rebuilt in a more elegant style. The heavy oak furniture was out of place in these surroundings and was replaced by lighter walnut pieces. However, an unusually severe winter of 1709 devastated the walnut trees throughout Europe. Seasoned stocks lasted until about 1720, which was all cut and exclusively used as a veneer. The tree was reintroduced to England in the mid-19th century. **Red**

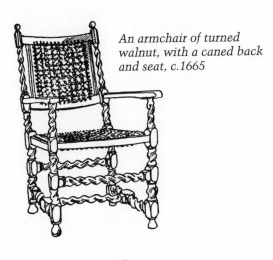

An armchair of turned walnut, with a caned back and seat, c.1665

walnut, or Virginian walnut (from the United States), is red-brown in colour and is often mistaken for mahogany. Susceptible to woodworm, very early walnut furniture is scarce today.

Mahogany. The carpenter on Sir Walter Raleigh's flagship during his voyage of 1595 to the West Indies and South America noted that he had seen mahogany trees, but it was not until 1733, when the high export duty on West Indian timber was repealed by Robert Walpole, that it became widely used. From that date, mahogany replaced walnut as the fashionable wood, and it remained the predominant wood for furniture throughout the 18th century. It was prized for its fine grain, figuration, and variations in density and colour range, from dark plum to light honey.

The first mahogany to be used by English cabinet makers was **Jamaican mahogany**. By 1745, however, supplies of this had been exhausted, and the importers went to Cuba as a new source. **Cuban mahogany** was marginally lighter, although often the figuring was superior. **San Domingo mahogany**, also known as Spanish mahogany, is denser and slightly darker and was considered better than Cuban mahogany. Its straight grain, and consequently greater strength, made it suitable for legs and other structural parts.

Honduras mahogany can have an interesting grain, sometimes known as 'feathering' or 'flame' pattern, but more often it is a plain, reddish-brown wood that fades in sunlight. It finally came into its own when stocks of other, better mahoganies were exhausted at the end of the 19th century. The dark **African mahogany** arrived in Europe in the 1830s, but was never used for high quality furniture.

As a general guide to dating a piece of mahogany, the closer the grain the older the piece.

Satinwood. The satinwood tree grows in both the West and East Indies. West Indian satinwood is a pale, clear yellow in colour. It was widely used as a veneer at the end of the 18th century by designers such as Thomas Sheraton (qv), for all manner of cabinet work and delicate pieces. East Indian satinwood is a much harsher, golden yellow colour, with a pronounced 'stripey' effect. Although it was known to the furniture makers of the late 18th century, it was rarely used. The first clue in identifying reproduction Sheraton pieces of c.1890–1920s is the use of this wood as a veneer.

Rosewood, so called from the smell of roses when it is felled, comes from both the East and the West. The East India Company imported rosewood – also known as blackwood, for its purplish-brown colour and black veining – from Sri Lanka and the eastern seaboard of India. It was used for cabinets during the Restoration. It was reintroduced to English cabinet makers after 1800, and was widely used until the end of the century. The better quality rosewood came from Brazil, hence its name **Rio Rosewood**. It is darkish brown in colour and distinguished by heavy black veining in attractive patterns.

As a general rule, during the 18th and 19th centuries mahogany was the preferred wood for the library and the dining room, while satinwood and rosewood were for the drawing room.

Ebony. The ebony used for veneering is very black, close-grained and hard. The tree, from the *Diospryros* genus, is grown in the tropical climates of Africa, Asia and America. The wood is grey or greenish-black in colour, with irregular portions of black appearing through the timber. It first appeared in France in the late 16th century and, because of the rarity and subsequent price of *ébène*, was only worked by the most skilled craftsmen who became known as *ébénistes*. The term stuck for those cabinet makers who worked in veneers, marquetry and inlays, as opposed to the *menuisier*, whose English equivalent was the carpenter or joiner. When ebony veneer went out of fashion in the mid-18th century, the two trades merged. Ebony was, however, still widely used for Boulle decoration (qv), and became fashionable again in France at the end of the 18th century with the Empire style. In England ebony was more commonly used for inlay, and as it was expensive it was often simulated by staining cheaper woods such as pine.

Elm was much used in country furniture. The planks could be cut far wider than oak, making it suitable for table tops, chair seats and, of course, coffins, but it is susceptible to woodworm attack. **Beech**, being in great supply, was another common wood for cheaper furniture. It was widely used for upholstered chairs, since it can withstand being nailed over and over again. **Sycamore** was useful for its whitish colour, which can be easily stained. It was popular for rustic pieces, particularly milk pails as the wood would not taint the milk. Many timbers were used for carcase work, **deal** (Scots pine) being the most common.

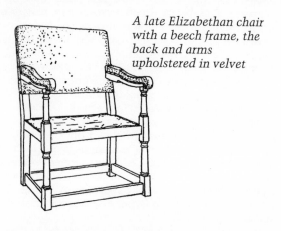

A late Elizabethan chair with a beech frame, the back and arms upholstered in velvet

THE GREAT FURNITURE DESIGNERS

Furniture styles are collectively named after the monarch in whose reign they are made, Elizabethan, Queen Anne, Georgian and so on, as they all follow the singular pattern that was in fashion at the time. However, from the late 17th century onwards designers and cabinet makers began producing furniture that owed more to their own creative skills than the general style of the period in which they worked. Such was their influence and originality, their pieces and designs carry their name. Many of the great designers and cabinet makers produced pattern books which were sold on subscription to lesser furniture makers. The cabinet maker's designs were thus extensively copied, so proliferating his work and immortalizing his name. Of the many fine designers of the 18th and 19th centuries, there are a few who have made a significant and lasting contribution to their trade.

Daniel Marot (c.1664–1752) was born in Paris the son of a famous architect and engraver. He also began his career as an engraver, and later made his considerable mark as an architect and designer of furniture. He was a Huguenot (French Protestant) and fled to Amsterdam in 1684, the year before Louis XIV revoked the Edict of Nantes (the treaty of 1598 whereby Henri IV had granted the Huguenots freedom of worship). Marot worked for Prince William of Orange, joining him in England on his accession as William III. He was responsible for much of the work at Hampton Court Palace. He published a book of his designs, *Oeuvres du Sieur D. Marot*, to keep the English abreast of French taste and fashion.

William Kent (1684–1748) was born in Yorkshire and apprenticed to a coach painter in Hull. He broke his contract and travelled to Rome to study painting. There he met the 3rd Earl of Burlington, who became his patron. The two returned to England where, fortunately, Kent turned from his meagre talents as a painter to his prodigious ones as an architect, landscape gardener and designer of furniture. Kent designed many of the great houses of the day, such as Houghton Hall in Norfolk, and was remarkable as the first architect to design an entire house, exterior, interior, furniture and furnishings, down to the smallest detail. His works were grandiose in the extreme: his style was Palladian (qv), with heavy festoons of flora and fauna, eagles and acanthus leaves. His was the 'English style', taking design away from the French influence of Marot. His school of landscape gardening was later exemplified by his friend and student Lancelot 'Capability' Brown. He was buried in Lord Burlington's vault at Chiswick Church.

Thomas Chippendale (c.1718–89). Little is known

about Thomas Chippendale's early life other than that he was born at Otley in Yorkshire, the son of a joiner and grandson of a carpenter. He came to London in 1749, and was living in St Martin's Lane by 1753. The following year, he published three volumes of *The Gentleman and Cabinet Maker's Director*, the first comprehensive trade work of its kind, which covered the three main styles associated with the elaborate and eclectic Chippendale – rococo, chinoiserie and Gothic (qv).

Although the concepts of the designs in the *Director* are certainly Chippendale's, he owed much to the work of his two draughtsmen, Matthias Lock and Henry Copland. Chippendale's workshops were small, with probably no more than 20 craftsmen, so the abundance of 'Chippendale' produced until the end of the 19th century was made by other hands faithfully copying designs in the book. The publication of the *Director*, a best-seller in its day, led to the creation of furniture not only for the aristocracy (although some of Chippendale's finest pieces are at Harewood House, Nostell Priory, Burton Constable and Newby, all in Yorkshire, and Paxton on the Borders), but also for the burgeoning middle class with money to spend on furniture. Chippendale's best work, especially his chairs of mahogany, then newly introduced from South America, dates from towards the end of his life, and is neo-classical in style. These designs may, however, have been influenced by the work of Robert Adams (qv).

Chippendale's son, another **Thomas Chippendale** (1749–1822), joined his father's firm and maintained it until after his death with his partner, Thomas Haig. His work can still be seen, like his father's, at Harewood House in Yorkshire and at Sir Richard Hoare's house Stourhead, in Wiltshire, which reflects the Regency taste of the period.

Robert Adam (1728–92). The renowned Scottish architect William Adam had four sons, all of whom practised in the family firm during the second half of the 18th century. Robert Adam was born in Kirkcaldy, Scotland and, after schooling in Edinburgh, travelled extensively in Italy and Dalmatia. There, between

*A design for a sideboard by Robert Adam, late
18th century*

1754 and 1757, he made extensive studies of Roman
antiquities that greatly influenced his development of
an elegant neo- classical style. He designed not only
buildings but all manner of furniture and furnishings
as well – chairs, tables, sideboards, cabinets, even fire
grates, door knockers, carpets and chandeliers – in this
neo-classical style. His designs were light and refined,
such as the delicate oval and shield backs to his
chairs. Much of his furniture was carved and gilded, or
painted. Single-handedly, he revolutionized English
taste in interior decoration. Among his most
important commissions were Osterley Park and Syon
House, both just outside London, and Kedlestone Hall
in Derbyshire.

George Hepplewhite (died 1786). Very little is
known of Hepplewhite, save that he was reputedly
apprenticed to the Lancaster firm of Gillow's, and that
he married a woman named Alice who continued his
business after his death. She published *The Cabinet
Maker and Upholsterer's Guide*, a posthumous work
of her husband's designs for furniture and furniture
ornaments. His style is considered to be a blend of
the rococo of Chippendale and the neo-classicism
of Adam. 'Chairs in general are made of mahogany,'

Hepplewhite wrote. 'Many of these designs are enriched with ornaments proper to be carved.' Typical are his shield and heart-shaped chair backs, decorated with swags, anthemion (honeysuckle), drapery, wheatears, and the three Prince of Wales feathers.

A girandole from Hepplewhite's The Cabinet Maker and Upholsterer's Guide, *1789*

Thomas Sheraton (1751–1806). Born in Stockton-on-Tees where he received a minimal education, Sheraton showed a natural artistic talent, and even taught himself drawing and geometry. The furniture of the late 18th century owes much to the influence of Sheraton, yet there is no record of him ever having owned a cabinet maker's workshop. He is credited with the publication of the *Cabinet Maker and Upholsterers' Drawing Book* in four parts in the 1790s, and of the *Cabinet Dictionary* in 1803. His *Drawing Book* summarizes the prevailing fashion of the neo-classical style. Fine satinwood inlay and veneer, straight lines and a delicate touch are the hallmark of pieces copied from Sheraton's books. Sheraton, a fervent Baptist, was ordained in 1800.

Thomas Hope (1769–1831). Born in London of a wealthy family, Hope's early years were spent travelling in Europe, Egypt, Greece, Turkey and Sicily, collecting marbles and making drawings of buildings and sculptures. His travels subsequently greatly influenced his own designs for furniture, made for his house in Duchess Street, London. These were reproduced in his work *Household Furniture,* published in 1807, and copied copiously by cabinet makers of the day. The originality of his designs lay in his close reproduction of Roman furniture, and with much classical and Egyptian ornament as decoration. The vogue for the Egyptian style in England during the first two decades of the 19th century can be attributed directly to him.

THE DECORATION

In his *Analysis of Ornament* written in 1855, Ralph Warnum states that 'Ornament is essentially the accessory to, and not the substitute of, the useful; it is a decoration or adornment'. Since the 4th century BC virtually all ornament has been basically a reinterpretation of the classical canon. The one marginal variation to this ornament was **arabesque**, which was common during the Renaissance in the 14th and 15th centuries (and periodically thereafter). Arabesque decoration is an intricate interweaving of flowing lines, curves and angles, either painted, carved or inlaid on furniture and plate. Its inspiration was classical, but Byzantine rather than directly Greek or Roman, and was developed in Islamic countries where it was forbidden to depict the human form.

A version of arabesque was used during the Tudor period, where it was called **mooresque**; it appears, surprisingly, around the rim of all Elizabethan communion cups. The similar **grotesque** motif is an exact copy of a frieze found at Nero's Golden House in Rome, excavated in 1500. A common motif of the Renaissance and beyond was **linenfold** (a 19th-century term), that resembled a linen sheet arranged in vertical folds. This was invented in the late 15th century and was carved on to wainscote wall panels, chests and presses. The style was not taken from folded linen but was a mannerist interpretation of the classical fluting of a column.

A major part of the classical revival from the 17th century onwards was the adoption of Graeco-Roman mythological symbols related to the pagan gods. These symbols, incorporated into all forms of interior decoration and furniture, were copied from the ornament of temples dedicated to the gods of the ancient world. The intention behind their use was to exemplify well-being in the home, as a place of everlasting spring, harmony, strength, plenty, festivity and, above all, love.

A silver-gilt fruit basket with stand, decorated with grapes and vines, 1811–12

The Roman god Bacchus, son of Jupiter (the Greek Dionysus, son of Zeus) gives rise to a host of classical motifs as the god of wine. He is represented by everything vinicultural, **grapes**, **vine leaves,** and **baskets.** He is also associated with feasting, often depicted seated in a carriage pulled by panthers (he also wears a panther's skin in war), and the motifs of the **panther's foot,** or hairy paw, and **panther's mask** are often found in dining room furniture. **Rams' horns and heads** are also Bacchic symbols connected with feasting and sacrifice. The most common of all classical motifs, the **eagle,** derives from a similar theme. In Greek mythology Ganymede, Zeus's golden boy, is cup-bearer to the gods and is represented riding an eagle.

Love is another common theme behind decorative motifs. Venus, the Roman goddess of beauty and sensual love, sprang from the foaming sea in a scallop **shell**, so fostering a range of nautical images. The shell is drawn by **dolphins.** The **hippocampus**, half horse, half dolphin, was the mount of Neptune, Roman god of the sea. Cupid, Venus's son by Mercury, Roman god of love, carries bows and, particularly, **arrows**. The **lion** symbolizes strength. Cupid riding a lion, or a pliant, passive, lion with a ring in its mouth, represents love's triumph over strength. The lion's **hairy paw** is another leonine symbol.

Although the Roman goddess Flora is associated with budding spring and **flowers**, she represents festivity, with motifs such as entwined **ribbons** and the **bucranium**, the sacrificed ox skull whose horns are decorated with a wreath. Another important goddess for classical motifs is Ceres, the Roman earth mother and protector of agriculture. She brings the **cornucopia** or goat's horn of plenty, overflowing with **fruit** and **corn**. Agricultural instruments, like the **plough,** are also attributed to her.

The ancient poets also created fantastic animals endowed with human attributes. The Greek **sphinx** had a recumbent winged lion's body with the bust and head of a beautiful woman, a form that was also adopted by the Romans and Egyptians.

Often the use of classical motifs was influenced by historical events. For example, with the popularity of all things French in the 18th century, the **dolphin** came to represent the *Dauphin*, the king's eldest son. In the late 18th and early 19th centuries the naval supremacy of Britain was reflected in the renewed use of the dolphin, and of **cannon** and **anchors**, while the **crocodile** was popular after Nelson's victory at the Battle of the Nile in 1798.

THE STYLES

Chairs, particularly dining chairs, can be readily dated by their backs and legs. The parts of a chair are all logical: the **toprail** or yoke rail runs along the top, the **stiles** or back uprights form either side, while the **splat** is the horizontal centre bar. Where the bars on the back are horizontal, they are termed **rails**. The **shoe** joins the splat to the back **seat rail** that holds the seat, and the horizontal struts that hold the legs in place are called **stretchers**.

DINING CHAIR BACKS

Turned, horizontal rails forming the chair back first appeared in the 16th century, and the style is descriptively called **ladder-back.** It became fashionable in the mid-18th century, when the rails became flat and serpentine-shaped. When the rail was pierced, it supposedly resembled the sound holes of a violin, hence the contemporary term 'fiddle-back'.

Fiddle-back was also the term used in the early 18th century for chairs whose side rails curved in to make the shape of a violin or fiddle. The **bended-back** chair with a baluster-shaped splat, introduced in the reign of Queen Anne, is thought to have come from the Orient. Its curved shape makes it extremely comfortable. With arms, the Victorians called it a 'Hogarth chair', as it appears in the artist's self-portrait and other paintings.

The classical Greek style adopted by mid-18th-century furniture makers was partially inspired by the four volumes of *Antiquities of Athens* published by the antiquary, architect and painter, James 'Athenian' Stuart (1713–83). The classical themes for the backs of dining chairs are all redolent of feasts and festivity. The delicate, carved **ribbon back** in the shape of entwined, silk ribbons, and the **wheat-sheaf back** with its waisted, pierced splat, were used by Chippendale in his most extravagant rococo designs of the 1750s.

Later in the 18th century came the **anthemion** or **honeysuckle back**, an oval back filled with the carved, curling petals of the honeysuckle. The **lyre** or **harp**

back of the same period resembles, as its name suggests, a stylized lyre or harp, inspired by the stringed instrument of Apollo, the Greek sun-god. The lyre signifies festivity and well-being.

The **shield back**, often containing the three ostrich plumes of the **Prince of Wales's feathers**, is associated with Hepplewhite and the last quarter of the 18th century. Hepplewhite produced many designs for the Prince of Wales, and would naturally have incorporated his patron's emblem where possible. The **balloon back**, shaped like a late 18th-century balloon (round at the top and tapering in towards the basket), was copied from the French, who called them '*Montgolfiers*' in honour of their famous balloonists.

Ribbon back   *Lyre back*   *Prince of Wales feathers*

A **rope** or **cable twist** appeared on the backs of chairs to commemorate Nelson's victory at the Battle of Trafalgar in 1805, and so they became known as Trafalgar chairs. At the same date, a black line in ebony inlaid into furniture was a sign of mourning after the death of Nelson.

CHAIR LEGS

The legs of 17th-century chairs and tables were usually turned, very often with a spiral, or **barley twist**, named after their resemblance to a stick of barley sugar. They were also known as **rope** or **double rope** twists. A **baluster** leg, which originated in the same period, is one turned in the form of a stone baluster.

A **cabriole** leg, or, as they were contemporarily known, **bandy** leg, curves outwards, then inwards, in a style copied by Dutch furniture makers either from a Chinese three-legged bronze cauldron, or from the legs of thrones found in ancient Greek theatres. The style came to England after the accession of William and Mary at end of the 17th century, and survived until the 1760s. The name comes from the French *cabrioler*, or the Italian, *capriolare*, meaning to gambol or caper like a goat, after its resemblance to the leaping animal's foreleg. The cabriole leg was replaced by the simpler **tapered** or **therm** leg in the second half of the 18th century.

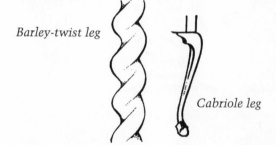

Barley-twist leg

Cabriole leg

The **clustered column** leg popular in the mid-18th century was taken from the Chinese and intended to simulate four bamboo sticks strapped together. Legs of the same period with a square section ending in a square plinth were called **Marlborough** legs, a tribute to the 4th Duke of Marlborough (brother of the Countess of Pembroke of the Pembroke table fame (qv)), to whom the cabinet makers Ince and Mayhew dedicated their book *The Universal System of Household Furniture* in 1762.

The klismos was an extremely elegant chair used by the ancient Greeks in the 6th century BC and portrayed on their vases and frescos. The design was revived during the late 18th and early 19th centuries. Its distinguishing feature is that it stands on the descriptively named **sabre** (or **scimitar**) legs, where both the front and the back legs curve outwards. After 1815 they became known as **Waterloo** legs, and later still as the less romantic **swept** legs.

FEET

One of the earliest symbolic feet to be used was the **animal paw** foot. These hairy paws, most commonly of lion, panther, or bear, appeared on stools and chairs in ancient Egypt, Greece and Rome, and in England from the Middle Ages. They came in and out of fashion frequently, as from the late 17th century to the mid-18th century, then again at the end of the 18th century for about 30 years. Where the hairy foot is a lion's, a lion's mask is often also used on the knee of the leg.

The furniture introduced to England in 1662 by Catherine of Braganza, wife of Charles II, had a distinctive scrolled foot called a **Braganza toe**. From the same period is the **Spanish** foot, also called a **paintbrush** or **tassel** foot which it resembles.

 *Spanish foot*

A highly decorative foot that was known in the late 16th century but came to greater prominence during the Restoration, and again from c.1720–60, was the **claw and ball** or **talon and ball** foot, taken from the classical eagle clasping a ball. It may also have originated from the Chinese motif of a dragon clasping a pearl in its claw. It was frequently used on a cabriole leg (qv).

Like the paw, the **hoof** foot is of ancient origin. Bull's cloven hoofs were carved in ivory on chair legs in the 3rd millenium BC, and goats' hoofs were common on Roman furniture. The cloven hoof came to English furniture makers from France (where it was known as a *pied de biche*) at the very end of the 17th century and remained popular throughout the 18th century, although the naturalistic hoof became more stylized by the end of the century. A satyr's mask often accompanied the cloven hoof on the knee of the leg.

The descriptive term **club** foot, like a plain pad, dates from the early 18th century. A refinement called a **pad** foot has a disc under the club foot. The **scroll** foot fashionable in the mid-18th century was also known variously as a **whorl** (scrolling outwards) and a **knurl** (scrolling inwards). Some were further embellished with carved acanthus leaves.

Fanciful adornments for feet, such as the head of a **dolphin**, or even the whole animal, were used by Chippendale in the mid-18th century and by Sheraton and Hope in the early 19th century. By the end of the 18th century, however, the absolutely plain **therm**, known more descriptively as **spade**, feet were more the fashion.

On cabinets and chest of drawers, the feet can give useful clues as to age, provided they are contemporary with the piece. These pieces have four distinct types of feet. The **bun** foot, rather like a flattened ball, was popular from the mid-17th century onwards. The plain **bracket** foot is made from two pieces of wood joined at the corner. The open side is decorated with a simple pattern, while the outer edge is straight. It was in use from about the late 17th to the mid-19th century. The late 17th-century **ogee bracket** foot is shaped with a double S-curve on both the inside and outside edges, while on the **splay bracket** foot of the late 18th century the line runs smoothly down the side of the piece and curves outwards at the foot.

CASTORS

As most furniture was designed to be easily moved, castors (small swivel wheels) were fixed to the legs of tables, chairs, and other larger pieces, particularly desks. Although there are rare examples of 16th-century castors, they were generally introduced in the late 17th century, and with the advent of heavy mahogany furniture in c.1730 they became essential. Early castors were simple affairs, a turned ball of laburnum (an extremely hard wood) mounted on a brass or iron axle. By 1750 these had been replaced by laminated leather castors, which were quieter and did not scratch the polished wooden floor. After 1770 castors were usually of solid brass, cast in the shape of the leg. As the tapered, square leg was replaced by a turned leg in about 1775, so the shape of the castor changed from box-shaped to round. Brass castors in the shape of a claw or hairy animal's foot were popular after 1800. Bronze castors were used on bulky or heavy furniture of all periods, while furniture with very durable white porcelain castors is undoubtedly Victorian.

HANDLES

Until the early 17th century most drawers and cupboards were opened by **wooden** knob handles or, if there was a lock on the door, by a key. These were then replaced by **iron hoops**, shaped like the key they replaced, with shaped iron back-plates, attached to the drawer or door by a form of brass or steel split pin called a snape. By the end of the 17th century brass handles had appeared. Their styles were generally copied from Europe, such as the Dutch **drop** handle. These were nearly always pear-shaped and might be finely decorated, for example with acorns. The back-plates were either simple discs or engraved quatrefoils. Another style of the period that survived into the 18th century was the **bifurcated (forked) drop** handle. At the turn of the century the **bail** handle was introduced, a 'C' scroll-shaped handle fixed to the drawer with a pair of snapes. After about 1710 the handle was held by a pommel, threaded at one end with a square nut, and a ball, drilled to take the lug of the bail at the other. The back-plate was of solid cast brass,often in a fanciful shape.

The **escutcheon**, the ornamented plate around the keyhole, usually matched the back-plate in design and form. Handles and escutcheons in the rococo style of the 1740s were wonderfully ornate, while by 1770 the style had become simpler again, with graceful swan-necked bails, initially on their own but later with a plain oval or octagonal back-plate. These back-plates were pressed out of sheet brass, which meant that they could be finely decorated in any style, like some nationalistic theme depicting one of Nelson's sea victories. After 1780 handles were fixed by round nuts. **Ring** handles in the neo-classical style, most commonly in the form of a lion's mask, appeared at the end of the 18th century. The wooden knob was reintroduced after 1820 and remained fashionable for the rest of the 19th century.

THE TYPES

TABLES

Tables can be divided into four distinct types: the dining table, the side table (to stand against the wall), the centre table (for fixed positions in the room away from the walls) and, from the 18th century onwards, the movable or occasional table, what the French called an *ambulante*, or strolling table.

DINING TABLES

The trestle table. Until the 16th century, the family and their servants dined together in the great hall of the house. They ate off simple tables made up from a few boards laid on top of collapsable trestles. These would be dismantled and stored against the wall after the meal so that the room could be used for other purposes. Food was served either on a shared wooden platter or trencher, or simply on a piece of stale bread that was afterwards thrown to the dogs or given to the poor. Trestle tables, usually made by the estate carpenter, remained in use for large dinners until the end of the 18th century. They would be made to size and covered with a damask table cloth.

The long table. The trestle table evolved in the course of the 16th century into a more permanent piece of furniture. The popular term 'refectory table' is a complete misnomer, as these ornate tables had little to do with the monasteries that were suppressed in the 1530s. These tables were made of oak, sometimes bog oak or even holly, and had wide tops supported on massive, bulbous legs, often ornately carved, joined at floor level by stretcher rails. They were made very long to accommodate the whole family and their guests. A more sophisticated variation, a **draw-leaf** table, had two leaves that pulled out from under the table top to increase its length. These were made throughout the Stuart period and, like the 'refectory' table, were much copied in the 19th century.

Falling or gate-leg table. By the early 17th century, the family and servants dined separately. The servants ate from plain, unadorned tables, usually of pine or elm, while the family and their guests dined at a falling table (the contemporary term for a gate-leg

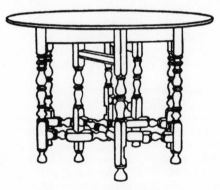

A gate-leg table

table) in their own 'eating room'. This table was usually oval, but occasionally round, with two hinged leaves hanging down beside the frame and eight legs, four fixed at each corner and four in the form of a 'gate' that swung out to support the two flaps. Like the trestle, the folded table would be removed from the room and stored after each meal.

Reproduction gate-leg tables were common throughout the 19th century, although one, the **Sutherland** table, was an original style from the 1820s. It was named after Queen Victoria's friend and Mistress of the Robes, Harriet, Duchess of Sutherland, who ordered the first table. This table is characterized by a narrow centre section and deep semicircular flaps, supported by two gates on the larger models, single legs on the smaller. The end columns are usually joined by a central stretcher. Because of the narrow centre section, the table can be folded away neatly against the wall.

An elliptical gate-leg table is often called an **Irish wake** table. The open coffin would rest on the central section of the table, and the narrow flaps would be opened out to take the glasses of the mourners. The elliptical shape is a common feature in Irish designs for all kinds of objects, particularly silverware.

The breakfast table. Gate-leg tables were refined during the 18th century, the cumbersome 'gates' being replaced by single legs, often finely carved cabriole legs (qv), to support the flaps, hence the term flap table, or breakfast table. In examples where the four delicate legs move to support the flaps, the table was appropriately described as 'spider-legged'.

Georgian dining table. Two tables with square ends would be put together when the occasion demanded, and later separate leaves were added between the tables. From there it was a short step to the Georgian dining table, with its central flap table, separate leaves and 'D' tables at each end. Like the trestle, this dining table was dismantled after use to make more space. The central flap table doubled as a breakfast table and the 'D' tables, known by Chippendale as 'round ends' or **compass** tables, were placed against the wall as console tables.

The pedestal dining table. By about 1780 the pedestal or, as it is sometimes known, the pillar dining table had become popular. Its central, turned column or columns meant that the sitter did not have to contend with the legs. The pedestal table developed from several tripod tables (qv) being joined together. Supported on either a tripod, or quadruple, spreading feet, these tables had either two or three columns, (with one or two additional leaves joined with brass clips) although there are examples of four, even six, column tables.

A useful way of dating pedestal tables is to look at the base of the column – if the legs come straight out in a smooth curve, then the table can be dated somewhere between 1780 and 1800; when there is a 'bump' between the legs and the column, then it is a later 19th-century table.

The patent dining table. Still with the idea that tables should be fully collapsable, ingenious 'patent dining tables' appeared in the 1790s. By cranking a handle, a small, compacted eight-legged table expanded into a dining table of whatever length was required with the addition of extra leaves. The northern firm of Gillow's produced a version that seated between '4 and 20 persons or any greater number' called an **imperial dining table**.

Victorian dining tables, like other pieces of large furniture, were little removed in style from those that had gone before, such as the refectory table or the patent dining table. Their versions, however, tended to be a great deal heavier. The novels of Sir Walter Scott influenced the design of tables in an 'Elizabethan' style.

SIDE TABLES AND SIDE FURNITURE

The original side table or **serving table** in the medieval hall resembled a long chest with a latticed front and a hinged lid, and set on stubby, square legs. It was used to rest food between the kitchen and dining table. Thereafter, the side table became an essential piece of furniture with an important function. At a time when people ate off wooden platters or trenchers, the family's silver and occasionally gold plate (the generic term for wrought metal) was piled on the **side table**, or buffet, as a display of wealth. The silver ewer, basin and cups used for washing hands at the table were placed on this table or board, which became known as a 'cup board'.

From the 16th century onwards, the side table became more elaborate and was shaped to accommodate a **wine cistern** underneath. This, made usually of marble, stone, or occasionally brass, was filled with ice, to cool the wine and then to wash the plates and glasses between courses. These arrangements survived with little change through the Tudor, Stuart and early Georgian periods, to the end of the 18th century.

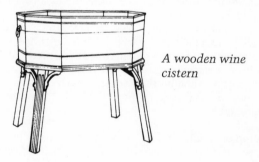

A wooden wine cistern

The 18th-century lead-lined box on legs, with a lockable lid, which held all shapes of bottles was called a cellar or **wine cellaret**, whereas a **bottle case** held square bottles only. At the end of the 18th century a lead-lined cooler of mahogany or occasionally rosewood, shaped like a **sarcophagus**, was much in vogue.

By the end of the 18th century the side table or side board, with the cistern below, was often flanked by two matching pedestal cupboards with a pair of urns above. The urns were either **knife vases**, to hold the tableware, or **wine fountains**, that held water to wash the plates between courses. They never held wine despite their name, although there are rare examples of table wine fountains of silver that did hold wine. These, however, were more for decoration as the silver tainted the wine. In the late 18th century the table, cupboards (qv) and urns were joined to make one piece of furniture called a **sideboard**, their amalgamation credited to the genius of Robert Adam (qv). This retained a shaped front for the cistern. Later the urns were removed, leaving a flat top with cupboards and/or drawers below. These drawers, also called **cellarets**, were often lead-lined to hold ice and water for rinsing glasses, or quartered to hold bottles or decanters in what was subsequently termed a **cellaret sideboard**. The cupboard often also housed a chamber pot. The **hunt sideboard** of the same period was higher, supposedly so that hounds in the dining room could not reach the food.

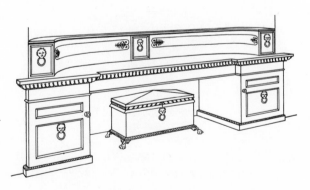

A sideboard with wine cooler, c.1810–15

The **side table**, designed to stand against the wall, was in use from the 15th century onwards. It was used in all reception rooms in grander houses, particularly the dining room, hall and drawing room. By the 18th century side tables had become primarily ornamental (although they did take candelabra and small decorative pieces), often intricately carved and gilded, and usually with a marble top – hence they were known as **marble** tables on the unromantically named **slab frames**. Travellers to Italy in the 18th century frequently brought back Roman mosaic to be made up as table tops.

A **console table** differs from a side table in that although it too stands against the wall it is permanently attached to it at the back and is supported in the front only by one or two scrolled bracket-shaped legs. Originally known as **clap** tables, they first appeared in the early 18th century and were often very ornate. The top was made of marble or **scagliola** – an imitation of marble or Florentine mosaic where the design is made from coloured, powdered marble set in cement – and the bracket legs richly decorated with motifs such as the eagle, or, much-favoured by William Kent (qv), the dolphin.

*A console table with a marble top and eagle support,
decorated with gilt gesso, c.1730*

The **pier table** was designed to stand against a pier, that is the part of the wall between two tall windows, below a pier glass (qv). These tables, similar to side tables in style and grandeur, often had marble tops so that the light from the candelabrum was reflected off the highly polished surface and the mirror of the pier glass behind. Early 18th-century pier tables were often made of gesso (qv). Commodes (qv) were sometimes used as pier tables.

CENTRE, MOVABLE, SPECIALIST AND TRIPOD TABLES

Centre tables. As its name implies, the centre table stood in the middle of the room, and was therefore designed to be seen from all sides. It was usually circular with a fine, decorative top, either of a figurative wood or inlaid. The pedestal base matched the period of the day. The **drum** or **capstan** table was popular from the mid-18th century. It is also circular on a pedestal base, and has a deep frieze containing a series of drawers. The round shape dictates that alternate drawers are dummies. Library models have a tooled leather top. A **rent** table is similar, but with a more solid base. It is a practical piece of furniture (some even have a slot in the centre to take the rent), with the drawers often marked with the names of the tenants or the letters of the alphabet.

Movable tables. The French invented the *table servante*, an ingenious table on wheels resembling the modern tea trolley, with a recess for bottles and decanters, a tray for glasses and a lead-lined well for ice. Louis XV's mistress Madame de Pompadour (1721–64) had one.

According to Sheraton (qv), the Countess of Pembroke (1737–1831) is credited as the lady 'who first gave orders for the **Pembroke** table, and who probably gave the first idea of such a table to the workmen'. She was Elizabeth Spencer, second daughter of the 3rd Duke of Marlborough. Although the shape of the top and the style may alter, the true Pembroke table is rectangular with two hinged flaps on the long sides. There is usually a drawer at one end and a dummy drawer at the other. It has always been a versatile item of furniture, serving equally well as a breakfast, tea or supper table. One particular adaptation was the **Harlequin** Pembroke table, developed from an ingenious invention of a Frenchman, David Roentgen, which combined a breakfast table with a ladies' writing table. By operating an internal mechanism with a key, the centre of the table could be raised or lowered to reveal a bank of small drawers with a series of pigeon holes. It was called a Harlequin table 'for no other reason but because, in exhibitions of that sort, there is generally a great deal of machinery introduced in the scenery'.

The **sofa** table was introduced soon after 1770 and differs from the Pembroke in that it is longer, the flaps are at each end and the drawers are in the frieze on one side. Early examples have four legs, later ones are on pedestals with either three or four feet or have bracket supports connected by a stretcher. The sofa table was an essential piece of drawing room furniture and was extremely popular in the Regency period. It stood either behind or in front of the sofa, to take a candelabrum. Like the Pembroke it was very versatile, and some are set with reversible chess and back-gammon boards or adapted for writing. The date of a sofa table can be determined by the height of the stretcher: the higher the rail, the earlier the table.

A sofa table

As the name implies, **trio** or **quartetto** tables are nests of three or four graduated tables that are stored one beneath the other. First introduced by Thomas Sheraton (qv), they had a multitude of uses. One was to take a jardinière, which when placed in front of the window, gave the impression of looking outside on to a flower-bed.

Specialist tables. Games and gambling have always been popular in England. A **pair of tables** was a medieval term for twin boards for chess or draughts on one side and 'tables', or backgammon, on the other. The specialist card table developed during the Restoration from these reversible boards, mounted on their own gate-legs. By the early 18th century card tables had a flap-top which was lined with baize and supported by a single fold-out leg. Later, when both the back legs moved out to support the top, it made for a sturdier table.

By 1720, an ingenious card table had been devised where half the frame with the two back legs 'concertina' (a modern term) out to support the baized top. Until c.1760 the top was often rounded at the corners and inset with four wells for money or counters. A late 18th-century card table with a circular top supported on a collapsible 'X' frame was known as a **commerce** table, after the popular card game of the time.

Even more economical with space were **double**, even **triple-purpose** tables. These mahogany semi-circular gate-leg tables had two or three flaps: turn over the first for a circular breakfast or supper table, turn over the second on its specially designed hinges for a green-baized card table. Under all three folds was a compartment for counters, cards and other oddments. The **pedestal card** table had a fold-over top that was pivoted slightly off-centre and turned through 90 degrees to rest firmly on its base. The style was in use from the mid-18th century to the end of the Regency. The **loo** table, of the same period, was large and circular and supported on four feet, designed specifically for the game 'lanterloo'.

Drawing, painting and letter writing were habitual occupations of the gentlefolk in the late 17th, 18th and early 19th century, and cabinet makers therefore made much specialist furniture for their purpose. For the artist and correspondent alike was the **drawing** or **architect's** table. Sturdy and of solid mahogany, it had an adjustable slope set into the top and operated by a ratchet, with compartments inside for brushes and paints. The writing slope could also be used to display pictures or act as a book rest. (For library tables see p.75 below.)

Needlework was another essential occupation for the genteel lady. The delicate **sewing** table appeared at the end of the 18th century, with a shallow drawer below. A **pouch** table or, as Sheraton described it, 'a Table with a Bag, used by the ladies to work at, in which they deposit their fancy needlework', had a top which often doubled as a chess board. The name **tricoteuse** for another small, ladies' work table with a gallery is the French word for 'a knitter', and alludes to those women who knitted in front of the guillotine during the French Revolution. The fashion for spinning also had to be catered for. Rather in the manner of Queen Marie Antoinette's model farm at Versailles, fashionable ladies would collect wool from the hedgerows to spin on delicate **spinning wheels**. These pretty drawing room pieces, of mahogany or satinwood veneer, with ivory fitments, were a far cry from the cumbersome machines of the professional spinners in the cottages. Very rare are hand-operated spinning wheels that were used on the lap.

A work table, c.1811

The **handkerchief** table of the mid-17th century was triangular when closed, to sit in a corner, and opened out to form a small square. From this developed the **envelope table**, which was square and doubled in size when opened. A small, useful Victorian folding table now known as a **coaching** table could well have its origins in 18th-century coaching travel. Certainly its shape, narrow and low, would fit between the seats of a carriage and the legs, hinged in the centre, could be folded neatly inwards.

Listed in the 1793 edition of *The Cabinet-Makers' London Book of Prices* (at 28s, or £1.40) is a design by Hepplewhite for a **gentleman's social table**. It is shaped like a large horseshoe and designed to be placed in front of the fire. There is usually a clever mechanism whereby a coaster bearing a decanter can travel round the table, either on a rail just below the narrow table top, or on an arm, pivoted at the centre. Some have a built-in fire screen, usually a curtain on a brass pole, to protect the drinkers from the heat. These tables were popular with Oxford and Cambridge dons, and with hunting families, hence its alternative (non- contemporary) name, **hunting** table.

Tripod tables and furniture. In 1660 the diarist Samuel Pepys wrote that he 'did send for a cup of tee (a China drink) of which I had never drunk before'. Tea and coffee had recently been introduced to England from Holland and were drunk by the wealthy in public tea and coffee houses. By the 1720s, the price of tea had dropped so much that dozens of tea-gardens opened up in and around London. When tea became widely available, the fashionable drank it at home. Thus, most furniture, ceramics and silver connected with tea date from that period onwards.

In the 18th and early 19th centuries tea was made in the drawing room. The hot water urn (qv), erroneously thought of as a tea urn, stood on an **urn stand**, a small, delicate table with four tapering legs and a square top with a wavy frieze. A slide or tray was pulled out to stand the teapot on. As tea was so expensive it was kept locked in a **tea caddy**, named after the Malay measure of weight *kati*, just over one pound. When the tea caddy was very large and supported on legs it was known as a **teapoy**. The term originally applied to a small rectangular table, with a pillar column on a tripod base, from the Regency period, and derived from the Hindi word *tepai*, meaning three-legged or three-footed.

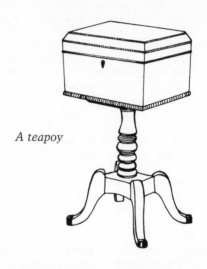

A teapoy

On most tripod tables (known contemporarily as **snap** tables) the circular, or sometimes rectangular, top is designed to be tilted vertically so that the table can stand against the wall when not in use. The top is set on a turned pillar (often on a device of turned stanchions, like a miniature playpen called a 'birdcage') and supported by three feet, to make it more stable on the uneven floors of the day. These were then known as **pillar-and-claw** tables. In dating tripod tables the pillar is the key element. On tables made before 1800 the pillar is fine, usually with a vase carved somewhere into the stem; after that date, the pillar is heavier, with a series of turned collars. Because of their popularity and usefulness, small, tripod tables have been widely copied, or converted from other pieces, such as pole screens (qv).

The most successful tripod tables are in mahogany, the only wood wide enough to take the width of the top in one plank, and easily carved. If the edge of the table is carved, for example with a pie-crust decoration, then it was meant to be seen and was called a **tea** table. If the edge of the table has a raised or fretted gallery, it is known as a **tray top** or **china** table, the idea being that valuable objects could not so easily be knocked off the table and broken. The lower **tea kettle stand** also has a gallery, better to hold the kettle and spirit lamp (qv). If the edge, pillar and feet of the table are plain it is a **supper** table, the unadorned table being designed to be covered by a linen cloth.

A rare version of the tripod table has four indentations in the top to hold a tray, usually silver, whose legs fit into the slots. With some tables of this type, the tray legs hung over the side. The tripod legs of an **Isle of Man** table are carved to depict a man's knee breeches and buckled shoes, an adaption of the island's coat of arms.

Other tripod tables that were essential in the 18th-century drawing room were the circular **wine** table (the term **occasional** table for any small table dates from the 19th century) that stood beside the chairs for wine glasses, and the **candle-stand** that was taller still. Candle-stands were also known as *guéridons*. Early *guéridons* sometimes took the form of a negro figure holding a tray, so-called after a famous Moorish galley-slave of that name. Guéridon was further immortalized as the character in a French song of 1850. Taller than the candle-stand was the *torchère* that also needed the steady tripod base for safety. Early *torchères* were known in the 17th century, usually made of oak. After the Restoration they were of ebony (for weight) and walnut, with twisted stems and a circular or octagonal top. Georgian candle-stands became very elaborate. Usually of mahogany, they were also carved, painted or gilded after the French manner, with vase-shaped tops and scroll feet.

In the 18th-century drawing room the main source of heat (and, to a lesser extent, light) was the fire. To protect the complexions of those sitting round an open fire, there were three types of fire screen. The **pole** or **stick screen** was introduced in the late 17th century and survived into the early 19th century. The movable screen was mounted on a slender pole, supported on a tripod base. Early oval or square screens were decorated with needlework panels, but by the 18th century were either solid or veneered wood, and sometimes shield-shaped. Some Regency fire screens had a banner on a pole mounted on a solid base. A **horse** or **cheval screen** had a larger panel, also worked in needlework, mounted on two uprights with two pairs of legs. The screen could be moved either up and down or forward and back like a cheval mirror (qv). Sometimes the screen had a collapsable shelf for writing, and was called a **writing fire screen.** Hand-held screens of **papier mâché** served the same purpose.

A most useful piece of furniture that dispensed with the need for staff in the dining room was the **dumb waiter**, a stand which first appeared in the 1720s. It had a central shaft on tripod legs with either three or four circular revolving trays, increasing in size towards the bottom. It was placed beside the table to carry all the extras needed for the meal. Versions with quadruple legs date from after 1800. A **Lazy Susan**, (the term is American) is a revolving tray that sits on the table to hold the condiments. Similarly, the **supper Canterbury**, a trolley with a tray on top, a shelf below and a semicircular end, was introduced for when servants were absent in the dining room or a meal was taken in the sitting room. According to Thomas Sheraton (qv) it was named after an archbishop who first ordered one, and it held 'knives, forks and plates at that end, which is made circular on purpose'.

Whatever its function, all furniture in the 18th-century dining room would be in a similar style. Everyday items such as a **plate bucket** or a **bone bucket** were finely turned in mahogany, with ribbed sides and brass-bound top and bottom. The only difference between them was that the plate bucket had a narrow slit down one side so that the plates could be removed singly, while the bone bucket (often mistermed a peat bucket) was for the rubbish left on the plates. Another useful piece of furniture was the **butler's tray**. This oblong galleried tray on a collapsible 'X' frame (called a voider) could be transported easily around the dining room. Later versions have hinged sides with carrying handles that fold flat when placed on the stand.

BEDROOM TABLES AND STANDS

The **dressing table** (a contemporary term) first appeared after the Restoration. This small table, of either walnut or oak, often had an adjustable mirror attached to the top and a series of drawers below for pots of powder, scent, combs and brushes, 'for rouging, painting and patching, for both men and women'. The table would be covered with a Turkey carpet or linen cloth known as a 'toilette'. Later the word toilet referred to the dressing table, then to the dressing room where it was placed, and finally to the activity of dressing and grooming. This function included the use of the **close stool**, a box with a tight-fitting lid to hold a chamber pot which was later transferred to a separate room. When water closets became common in the late 19th century, the room kept its original name, toilet.

The dressing table was refined by the Georgian cabinet makers, in particular Thomas Sheraton (qv). The top opened up to reveal a mirror on a slide, sometimes with movable mirrors on each side as well, and a myriad of tiny compartments for powders and pins, pomades and scents. A knee-hole dressing table is similar to a sideboard (qv) save that a dressing table has four legs and a sideboard generally has six or more.

The **basin stand** was a delicate piece of bedroom furniture in the mid-18th century. A porcelain bowl was set into a circular top, supported on three uprights with tripod legs. In the centre was a shelf for the soap dish, and beneath it a drawer for other toiletries and a final shelf for the ewer at the bottom. These stands are often mistaken for **wig stands**, which date from the 17th century. Wigs were hung on the tops of turned stems, either singly or in pairs. Another bedroom piece resembling a miniature snap table (qv) is the

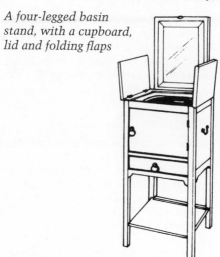

A four-legged basin stand, with a cupboard, lid and folding flaps

watch stand, designed to hold a hunter watch at night.

A Regency variation of the basin stand was the **wash-hand stand**, a chest, often with a marble top, designed to accommodate a 'toilet set' – a larger bowl, ewer and toothbrush jar. The mid-18th-century **wash-hand table** resembled a chest of drawers, but the top opened to reveal a basin fed from a small water tank behind. A **shaving** table was similar, but with the addition of an adjustable mirror. The **bed** table, similar to the modern breakfast tray, was an 18th-century invention.

CHAIRS AND SOFAS

In the medieval household stools and benches were the most common forms of seating; only the most important, the head of the family or the guest of honour, sat in chairs (hence the term 'chairman') which evolved from the chest. Initially, the lid was the seat, while the back and sides were extended to head height to form what became known as a **settle**. The sides of the chest then disappeared leaving four legs, and the side panels above the seat were refined into arms. Until the 16th century these chairs had arms and were called **armed** or **arming** chairs. Chairs without arms developed from the joint stool (qv). Known as a **back-stool**, the back legs of the stool were extended upwards and joined at the top by a rail.

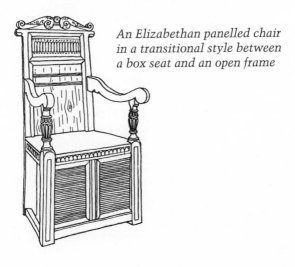

An Elizabethan panelled chair in a transitional style between a box seat and an open frame

Similarly, the **X-chair**, a common medieval chair, developed from the folding stool (qv). Designs differed according to use, and styles developed over time.

STOOLS, DINING AND SIDE CHAIRS

The most common early form of seating was the **joint** or **joyned** stool with turned legs made of joint construction. The Victorian term for this, coffin stool, is incorrect as coffins generally stood on trestles not stools, although Samuel Pepys does write in 1661 of his uncle's coffin 'standing upon joynt-stooles'. Another form of stool was the **X** or **folding** stool, a design dating from the 2nd millennium BC and used by the ancient Greeks and Romans. The frame is a simple 'X', with either a solid or canvas top. The design returned in the 18th century as a ladies' **dressing** stool.

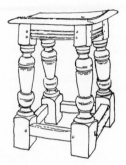

An oak joyned stool, mid–17th century

The medieval **footstool** formed part of the throne or chair of state, and would later match upholstered armchairs. By the mid-19th century it had become very elaborate, and might serve more than one purpose – some had a concealed spitoon under a hinged lid, known by the Victorians as a salavarium! The **tabouret** was another upholstered stool, introduced from France in the early 17th century, where only certain ladies of rank at the court of Louis XIV could be seated on them. **Gout** or **gouty** stools of the 18th century were either adjustable in height or richly upholstered to support a painful leg.

The Ottoman footstool of the early 19th century had a stuffed top, usually buttoned (qv), and stood on four feet, usually of rosewood or mahogany. It was large enough to double as a fireside seat.

Because of their method of construction (pegged mortise and tenon joints) oak dining chairs changed little in shape or design until the advent of walnut furniture after the Restoration. After the richness of the early Stuart period the Puritan austerity of the Commonwealth brought much greater simplicity. The new style was for a simple, armless chair, with turned front legs, the seat and back upholstered in leather nailed to the frame with bright brass studs. The term **Cromwellian** or **Puritan** for chairs is descriptive rather than contemporary. The moustachioed, bearded figure carved on the shaped and scrolled backrail of the **mortuary** chair is supposed to portray Charles I. Regional chairs adopted a similar design but without the carving, and were known as either **Yorkshire** or **Derbyshire** chairs. All these chairs were widely copied in the late 19th and early 20th century.

Until the middle of the 17th century dining and side chairs were virtually one and the same thing. After the Restoration, the two remained similar in shape, size and design, but side chairs acquired upholstered backs and, if they had them, upholstered arms as well. Also at this time caning became popular for both dining and side chairs. The canes were imported from the Malay peninsula in great quantities by the East India Company. **Caned** chairs and day-beds were quick and inexpensive to make, and were particularly popular after the Great Fire of London in 1666 which destroyed so much furniture in the city. At this time the motif of carved cherubs supporting the royal crown (known as 'boys and crown') was common on toprails of chairs, possibly to suggest the happy restoration of Charles II.

In the wake of the Glorious Revolution of 1688 and the accession of William and Mary came Dutch fashion in both dress and furniture. Women wore high mantillas and combs in their hair, and this style was reflected in the furniture, particularly in the **high backed** chair, whose back was two-and-a-half times the height of the seat. These chairs were lighter than the regional chairs of the day and, with their disproportionately high, spindly backs, were far from strong. The tops of the chairs were usually ornately carved, which gave rise to their later name of **periwig back.**

Another important innovation to come from France by way of Holland was a totally new design of chair 'in the style of Daniel Marot' (qv). Marot's chair, with its narrow back and vase, or fiddle-shaped splat (qv) supported on cabriole legs (qv), was to set the fashion for the next century.

During the 18th century guests and family sat in no particular order at table except that the most senior men, the head of the family and important guest, were expected to carve and sat in the most comfortable chairs, with arms. They became known as **carvers**. On a **mess** chair the left arm is missing, but although the sword is worn on the lefthand side officers do not wear them when dining in the mess so this name is misleading. If the carver genuinely belongs to a set of chairs, the front seat rail will be a little wider than on the other dining chairs. If the rail is the same width, the arms have been added at a later date.

The styles of dining and side chairs changed markedly throughout the 18th century, particularly in the width and shape of the splat, the central upright of the chair back. The broad splat of the Queen Anne chair back became narrower and more refined by the decade, until the advent of the delicate carved and pierced splats from the likes of Chippendale (qv) during the mid-18th century. Towards the end of the century, Thomas Sheraton (qv) introduced the chair back with vertical, separated splats. The side and dining chairs of the Victorian era are characterized by rounded and balloon backs.

A typical dining chair of c.1850

OTHER NON-UPHOLSTERED CHAIRS

Decoration of the simpler chairs of the 16th and 17th centuries was left to the wood turner, who produced **turned-all-over** chairs. The seats were triangular and everything else – legs, struts, backs – was turned.

Bobbin-turned chairs were decorated with wooden rings, more for decoration than comfort.

A chair designed to be particularly uncomfortable in the 18th century was the **hall** chair. These stocky, solid chairs, usually with the crest or the arms of the family painted on the back, were placed around the hall for the benefit of the servants, or for visitors not grand enough to be received in the reception rooms. They were also placed outside each reception room and the principal bedrooms for attending footmen. In grander houses and gentlemen's clubs, there was always at least one servant permanently on duty in the hall to open the front door and help guests in and out of their carriages; he was fortunate to have the comparative comfort of a **porter's** chair. Generally leather-covered and studded, it resembled a domed sentry box and was designed to keep out the draughts of the hall.

The charming story that a **Windsor** chair was so named after George III saw one when sheltering from the rain in a butcher's cottage in Windsor is apocryphal, as the first documented reference to a Windsor chair pre-dates the birth of the king. It is more likely that as the centre of their manufacture was Chepping (High) Wycombe in Buckinghamshire, the chairs arrived in London from Windsor. There were many regional variations on the chair, from Somerset to Lancashire. Whatever their provenance or nomenclature, their arrival dates from the turn of the 17th century, and they have been made ever since.

Windsor chairs were invariably made of a stick-back construction. The spindles in the back, like the legs, were of either beech or ash, turned by 'bodgers' working in the woods and sold in bundles to village chair makers. A variety of woods were used in the rest of the construction. The seat was usually elm, and worked into a saddle shape by a 'bottomer' using an adze, a hand-held tool like a miniature hoe. The frame was generally yew. The chairs can be either low or high-backed. The low-backed chairs were similar to the writing chair (qv), with a curved yoke for a back rail. The high-backed chairs, generally of a later date, had two variations: 'comb-back' with a straight rail

*A hoop-back
Windsor chair,
early 18th century*

and spindles resembling a comb, and 'hoop-back' with a curved top rail. The legs were either cabriole (qv) or turned, while some had beautifully curved stretchers. During the 1760s, the Windsor chair was produced in the Gothic style. Even the Prince of Wales's feather motif was used towards the end of the 18th century. Chairs made to be used outside were painted, usually green, but also red or black.

A chair more associated today with America than England is the **rocking** chair. Its design is credited to the American statesman, Benjamin Franklin, in the 1760s, surprisingly late as rockers had been common on babies' cribs since the Middle Ages. The early chairs were ordinary rustic chairs with ladder-backs (qv) and rush seats, or plain Windsor chairs with rockers attached, but they developed with a better design in the United States where manners were more relaxed than in Georgian and Victorian England.

UPHOLSTERED CHAIRS

Until the 15th century upholstery was little known. 'Upholders' covered chairs with leather or cloth which was either draped or nailed in place. Quilted material (qv) was often just tied on to the chair with ribbons, more to hide the chair and show off the cloth, than for comfort. Squab (flat, sewn) cushions made them more satisfactory. The early 17th-century chairs, known contemporarily as **upholsterers'** or **imbrauderers'** chairs were stuffed with a soft material such as straw, feathers or horsehair. Sold in sets, they could also be hired from the upholsterer for larger parties.

The **farthingale** chair, or back-stool, of the same period had no arms and an extra-wide seat. The name suggests that it was designed for women who wore huge metal hoops in their petticoats, known as farthingales, which is probably true, but the term was only coined by the Victorians. The chairs were covered in velvet, damask, or Turkey work (qv). The covering was fixed by large brass-headed nails on to braid, often with a fringe as well. Upholstered stools remained popular right up to the end of the 19th century, particularly during those times when voluminous skirts were the fashion.

The basic method employed in upholstering chairs in the Restoration altered little until the invention of the coil spring in the mid-19th century, although the technique was refined and improved throughout the 18th century. A lattice of webbing of woven hemp was nailed to the bottom of the chair. A linen-covered 'sausage' filled with hay or straw, wool, horsehair or feathers, was nailed on to the inside front edge of the frame to form a well with the back of the chair. This was then filled with horsehair held in place by a linen or canvas cover, before the final covering of velvet, silk, damask or other fabric, was nailed down. There was a vogue at this time for loose covers, but it did not extend much beyond 1730. The main breakthrough in upholstery came with the introduction of the spring. Patents had been taken out for a spring as early as 1707, but it was not until the 1830s that they were universally employed in all seat upholstery.

Until the second half of the 18th century the only method of attaching fabric to a chair was simply to stretch it over the upholstery and secure it with nails at the edge. The invention of **buttoning** provided an alternative. Originally an ornamental device, buttoning was soon found to be practical and hardwearing, particularly for the interiors of coaches and sedan chairs. The seat and back were upholstered in the normal way, then leather- or cloth-covered buttons were pulled in tightly from the back with strong thread, giving a bulging effect. Buttoning is always done in a regular pattern, usually diamonds but occasionally squares.

Tall, folding screens and easy chairs were used from the end of the 17th century onwards to combat the ever-present cold draughts. The term 'easy chair', now applied to every upholstered armchair, is, in fact, contemporary. They are also known as **lug** or **wing chairs**, from the 'wings' that extend from the back for extra protection. A refinement was the **saddle cheek** chair whose wings resemble the back of a saddle. The terms **draught** or **grandfather** chairs are late Victorian, the latter having the same source as the grandfather clock, a line in a popular American song of 1878.

Women's chairs tended to be lower and smaller than men's. The mid-18th-century women's armless **nursing** chair was only 13 inches off the ground. So too was the **ladies'** chair of the Regency period, with its seat and back rail made in a continuous sweep. It was the forerunner to the **Spanish** chair, which was slightly more padded.

Another common style of arm, or elbow, chair, with an upholstered seat and back and with open sides was known in the mid-18th century as a **French** chair (the name Gainsborough chair is modern). Upholstered in leather or damask, it had a broad seat to accommodate the fashions of the day – the wide skirts of both men's waistcoats and women's dresses. The Victorians, ever censorious of the supposed licentiousness of the Georgian era, called them **drunkards'** chairs, in the belief that drunks could better loll on their broad seats.

A ladies' elbow chair in the same style in the late 18th century was called a **Martha Washington**, named after the American president's wife who owned something similar at Mount Vernon. The upholstered chair has a neatly tapered, high back with a serpentine curved top, open arms and a shallow seat. (A Martha

A Martha Washington chair

Washington table, named on the same premise, is a sewing table with rounded ends and compartmented drawers for sewing implements.)

In the mid-18th century, the original **bergère** chair was a semi-reclining chair with an elongated seat and high back (a similar, padded Victorian version was called a 'lounge'). By the end of the 18th century the bergère was an upright chair with a much smaller, caned seat and back. With upholstered arms, or pads on the arms, this becomes a *fauteuil*. The mid-18th-century **conversation** chair, or *voyeuse* as it was originally called in France, was similar to a bergère but with the addition of a padded 'shelf' across the back. Spectators of card or other games of chance could either lean on the chair back in comfort without disturbing the player or, as with the English version, according to Sheraton (qv), 'the parties who converse with each other sit with their legs across the seat, and rest their arms on the top rail, which, for this purpose, is made about three and a half inches wide, stuffed and covered'.

The same mode of sitting applied to the **reading** chair of the early 18th century, where the reader straddles the leather upholstered chair the 'wrong way round', that is with legs astride the narrow back, and forearms resting on the top of the upholstered, semi-circular back. Most have an adjustable flap to write or

69

rest a book on, some have a swing drawer under the arms for bottles of ink and pens. There is often a drawer under the seat for papers. The library chair has wrongly been called a cockfighting chair from its appearance in contemporary sketches of cockfights.

There were two versions of the **writing** chair in the early 18th century. One had elbow arms that sloped back so that the chair could be drawn up close to the desk or writing table, the other, also called a **corner** chair, had one leg at the front and back, and two legs in the middle. The front was bowed, the back curved inwards.

Club chairs of the 19th century were deep and well upholstered for members to snooze in after luncheon. A **smoker's** chair was similar but distinguished by a drawer containing a spitoon under the seat.

LARGER UPHOLSTERED FURNITURE

Although first introduced in the late 16th century, the **day-bed** only increased in popularity after the Restoration. Placed at the bottom of the bed, or elsewhere in the bedroom or sitting room, it was where the mistress of the house received her guests in the daytime. These day-beds were generally of carved walnut with a caned seat and an adjustable back operated by a series of hooks and chains, supported on six or eight legs. The earlier beds had a stuffed squab cushion or mattress, which was replaced by permanent upholstery towards the end of the 17th century. The **Knole sofa**, a double-ended day-bed whose arms could be lowered or raised, was named after the one made for the famous house in Kent early in the 17th century. It was much copied in the 1920s.

The term day-bed and couch were interchangeable in the 17th century. By the 18th century, the many forms of couch were used primarily for lolling in comfort, in either the bedroom or private sitting room. The couch has a high back to support the head and two padded arms. The French model, called a **_péché-mortel_**, sometimes came apart in the middle to form an easy chair and stool; when another easy chair was added at the end it became a **_duchesse_**. Sheraton

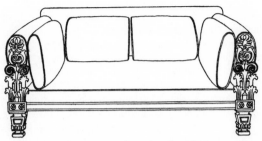

A Grecian style sofa of c.1830

produced an elaborate 'duchess bed' complete with a collapsible canopy on movable posts. The ***chaise longue***, a couch with a scrolled back and sides, was copied from the French in the mid-18th century. The back of the similar Grecian squab of the early 19th century reached halfway up the back of the sitter.

The word **settee** was in use a little before **sofa** or sopha in the 18th century to describe a seat with arms for two or more people. The settee developed from the settle, while the word sofa comes from the Arabic *suffa* meaning an Asian alcove or according to Baily's *Dictionarium Britannicum*, 'an apartment of state, raised from about half a foot to two feet higher than the

A typical sofa of c.1860

floor, and furnished with rich carpets and cushions, where honourable personages are entertained'. The **bar-back** or **chair-back** settees of the late 18th century have upholstered seats with usually two or three, sometimes more, chair backs of the current style joined together for the back.

The 4th Earl of **Chesterfield** (1694–1773), statesman and diplomat, gave his name to an overcoat and probably also to a large, double-ended overstuffed sofa. This sofa, however, was not manufactured until 19th century.

CUPBOARDS, BOOKCASES, DESKS AND CHESTS

DINING ROOM AND SIDE CUPBOARDS

The **buffet**, or large side table, of the 16th century had two or three shelves above and below the board to display extra plate. When one or more of the shelves was enclosed it was known as a **court** or **press cupboard**. When drawers were placed under the board and shelves were added above, it was known as a *dressoir* or **dresser**, where the food was 'dressed'. A **Welsh** dresser has the doors at the bottom, a **Yorkshire**

A carved oak cupboard in two tiers, late 17th century

dresser has a clock somewhere in the piece, a **Lancashire** dresser has a breakfront, and an **Irish** dresser has a latticed front to hold laying hens.

DRAWING ROOM AND LIBRARY CUPBOARDS

Since medieval times possessions have been displayed as a show of wealth. The popularity of drinking tea and coffee from the Restoration onwards led to the importation of Oriental porcelain and the subsequent need for a suitable cupboard in which to store and, more importantly, to display it. These early **china cabinets** were lacquered; thereafter they followed the decorative style of the day.

Although not introduced until the end of the 18th century, a particularly useful piece of furniture for the Victorian collector of small decorative items was the **what-not**. Designed to stand against the wall, it had three, four or five shelves supported on slender uprights. Later versions were made triangular to fit a corner. Heavier what-nots were known as *étagères*, the same name as was given to 18th-century hanging wall shelves also used for displaying trinkets.

The French *chiffonier* was a tall chest of drawers, while a *chiffonière* was a small set of drawers on legs where ladies put their unfinished needlework and *chiffons*, scraps of cloth. The piece was copied in England in the late 18th century. The Regency **chiffonier** was a low cupboard with shelves above for books or ornaments.

A typical early 19th-century piece was the **Wellington chest**, designed for the collector of coins, birds' eggs or other small articles. This had between six and twelve thin drawers, and a lockable side flap that hinged over to secure them. To describe any new piece of furniture as 'Wellington' or 'Waterloo' was popular among furniture makers after 1815.

DESKS AND BOOKCASES

The passion for correspondence that began with the Restoration reached its height in the 18th and mid-19th centuries, and furniture designed specially for the letter writer kept pace with the vogue. The desk (a medieval term) developed from the simple **writing box** of the 16th century. Misnamed by the Victorians as a Bible box, this had a hinged lid on the slope and compartments inside for papers and ink. These early, portable writing boxes rested on a table and when towards the end of the 17th century, box and table were joined into one piece of furniture the result was the **bureau on stand**. When this writing box 'married' a chest of drawers, the **bureau**, or desk, as it is known today was created. The term bureau comes from the word 'bure', a coarse woollen cloth (baize) used for covering writing boards.

A scrutoire

The **scrutoir** developed from the Spanish *vargueño*, a writing chest fitted with a series of drawers and pigeon holes and a fall front side to write on. It was placed either on a table or a stand. It was popular during the Restoration, and was usually made of walnut.

Every 18th-century library would contain some form of writing or library table. The most common was the **pedestal desk** or **writing table**. This was a large, flat-topped desk with an inset leather top, standing on two pedestals with either drawers or cupboards on one side. When the desk could be used on both sides at once, it was called a **partners' desk**. Although very large, these library tables were often fitted with carrying handles. A small writing table with a superstructure of drawers and a cupboard was called a *bonheur-du-jour*. Set on tall legs, these were introduced from France in the 1760s, but were never very popular. Occasionally they were fitted with compartments for holding toiletries or for displaying ornaments.

A smaller knee-hole desk, variously called a **bureau table** or **library writing table** appeared towards the end of the 18th century. Circular, even kidney-shaped library tables appeared under the influence of Sheraton (qv) and Hepplewhite (qv). Some were embellished with writing slides that pulled out to allow more than one person to use the table, others had pull-up reading slopes. By the Regency, some library tables even had a circular bookcase in the centre.

On 22 July 1666 Samuel Pepys noted in his diary that 'Simpson the joiner and I spent all day with gt. pains contriving presses to put my books in'. Although there are examples of medieval **bookstands** most date from the Restoration. After that date, bookcases in libraries began to be built in, and the bookcase itself was often combined with another piece of furniture, as, for example, in one of the most useful pieces of furniture of the mid-18th century, the **bureau bookcase,** or 'Desk and Bookcase' as Chippendale described it. The bookcase above the desk was usually enclosed by mirrored doors with a slide, often two slides in the form of a small pull-out tray, to support a candlestick in front of the glass. The light was then reflected off the mirror. The writing flap folded forward and was supported on slides. Of the same period is the **secretaire bookcase**, which differs from the bureau bookcase in having a dummy drawer fitted out with drawers and pigeon holes that pulls forward and is self-supporting. At the end of the 18th century, when French terms were unfashionable, this piece became known as a secretary drawer.

The **tambour**, a cylinder-top writing-desk, the forerunner of the roll-top desk so beloved by the Victorians, appeared at the end of the 18th century.

On the cylinder-top desk the curved panel was in one piece, whereas the later roll-top was created from a series of shaped slats, glued to a strong canvas, running in grooves on either side of the semicircular top. The term 'tambour' also applies to sliding doors of the same period, often seen on pot cupboards.

In about 1790, a certain Captain Davenport instructed the Lancashire firm of Gillow's to make him the small, travelling desk and chest to take to India, which subsequently became known as a **Davenport.** Whether or not the desk was really named after him is unknown, as desks of this type were known before that date. It was a clever design, where the writing slope slid forward to allow room for the sitter's knees, a slide pulled out for papers on the side, while under the writing slope were many drawers for the storage of inks, pens and papers. The design was later adapted and the piece became an essential part of Victorian drawing room furniture.

At the end of the 18th century, the Prince of Wales is said to have approved the designs for a desk by Henry Holland for Carlton House, his London residence. The **Carlton House writing table** is 'D'-shaped, with drawers in the deep frieze and a row of drawers and pigeon holes curving across the back and round to the front, topped with a brass gallery.

BEDROOM CHESTS

The **chest of drawers** developed from a simple oak chest. The carcase was made of heavy boards pegged together with a hinged lid on top. It was used to store the family's valuables, plate, linen and clothes. It also doubled as a bench seat. By the Tudor period, the chest, by now often ornately carved, was known variously as a marriage chest, linen chest, or dower chest. When chests were made with short legs, like the **mule chest** of the 1650s, the next step was to fit a drawer between the legs to create a 'chest and drawer'.

By the Restoration the chest of drawers had fully evolved into a set of drawers, the grander being veneered in walnut. Usually these were set on stands; from the 18th century they sometimes rested on other

76

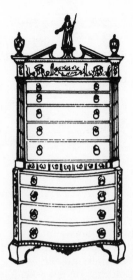

A tallboy

chests and the piece became known as a **chest-on-chest** or **tallboy.** As a rule, the drawers on a tallboy were graduated, with the deepest on the bottom, narrowing towards the top. The top drawer might be split into two, even three, small drawers. This made sense, as the higher the drawer the lighter it needed to be when pulled out overhead. In the early 19th century, when the chairs that had traditionally been placed around the walls were repositioned in the room, there was room for more furniture in the drawing room. Often bedroom furniture, being the only spare furniture in the house, was taken downstairs. Tallboys were split, the upper half being put on bracket or bun feet, and the tops, formerly out of sight and therefore plain, were veneered.

During the 18th century chests of drawers were made in many styles and shapes, either straight, bow-fronted or serpentine. Often the drawers had extra functions, such as the secretaire drawer that pulled out for writing, or a drawer resembling a dressing table with a ratchet mirror and compartments for other toiletries. A particularly useful small chest of drawers was the **lobby chest.**

*A serpentine- fronted chest of drawers, late
18th century*

This had four drawers and a fold-over top lined with
baize that served as a dressing or writing table. It often
also had a pull-out slide, known as a 'brushing slide',
not for brushing clothes on (as is widely held) but for
putting hair brushes on as a dressing table, or of course
for writing on. It was originally placed on the passage
side of enfilade rooms (those leading one into another),
so they had to be narrow. The name bachelor chest
for a lobby chest, though now in use, is not a
contemporary term.

The **commode** came to England from France in the
mid-18th century. The French commode differed from
the chest of drawers it resembled in having a shaped
rather than flat front, either serpentine, semicircular,
or elliptical. Some English versions had doors rather
than drawers, or sometimes both. They were made for
the bedroom but, being ornate and decorative, they
also made their way downstairs to the drawing room.
The Victorians, with characteristic prissiness, misnamed the 19th-century close chair incorporating
a chamber pot, a commode. An essential piece of
furniture in the 18th-century bedroom was the **pot
cupboard** that housed the chamber pot, often incorporating a **close stool** or night commode, a simple
box stool with a hinged lid, below.

BEDS

The Romans devised the ultimate bed, which has still to be improved upon. The patrician was rocked to sleep by a slave on the 1st-century equivalent of a waterbed and, when asleep, was moved to an ordinary mattress on the other side of the bed.

In the 11th century, the rudimentary windows in even the grandest houses were so ineffectual in keeping out the cold that beds were built against the wall like small rooms, or into alcoves known as bed-closets or bed-coves. Heavy curtains or shutters then made these **shut-beds** relatively draughtproof. The bed-case was a simple frame laced with bed-lines (strong cord) to support the bedmatt, a woven straw or rush mat to support the bedding or straw-filled pallet. A great luxury was the feather bed, where the pallet was filled with goose feathers. When the bed-lines began to sag, a wooden spindle was used like a tourniquet to tighten them, and this is the origin of the expression 'sleep tight'. This spindle was useful as a **bedstaff**, and used to smooth the sheets when making the bed.

The later **stande** or **wainscot** bed was still built like a small room, with panelled head and foot boards, a tester canopy on top, and the sides formed by curtains. Alternatively the tester was supported on the headboard and two posts at the foot, the two sides and end enclosed by spavers (bed curtains). Often, the tester with curtains was suspended from the ceiling. In grander beds a feather, hair or cotton-filled mattress replaced the pallets. A **truckle** bed, a smaller bed fitted with wheels and stored under the main bed during the day, was for children, page boys, or servants.

In all ages the bed was a very important and expensive possession which was invariably specified in a will.

Little changed in bed design until the late 17th century, when the bedchamber took on a new importance. As there was better protection against draughts and the cold, necessity gave way to decoration. The solid back panel and canopy were replaced by richly carved bedposts, supporting a wooden cornice from which to hang the bed curtains.

Although the term was current in medieval times the **state** bed for the accommodation of princes and noblemen is more associated with the 17th and 18th centuries. Apart from its size and grandeur, what distinguishes a state bed is that all the woodwork – the posts, headboard and tester – is covered with the same fabric as the curtains. These beds would be in the current style, whether an **angel** bed or **half-tester** (a 15th-century design where the tester covered a quarter of the bed) or a **dome** bed, where the tester is dome-shaped.

During the 18th century the great designers produced all manner of beautiful and ingenious beds. Although similar in design, the bedposts and hangings became lighter, usually reeded and cylindrical in shape, carved with a variety of designs such as wheat-ears, acanthus leaves, or a vase on a square base. Chippendale produced a **couch** bed in the rococo style, which resembled a couch with wonderful hangings from an overhead dome.

There is no evidence to support the story that a **Marlboro'** bed, a heavy, mahogany four-poster, was adapted from the field bed used by the 1st Duke on his campaigns. The bedposts on a **tent** or **field** bed were no more than five feet high, and the hangings were suspended from a curved, iron tester rail. They were popular for single women and so named for their similarity in size and shape to those used in camps. At the end of the 18th century, Thomas Sheraton (qv) designed a pair of single beds 'to keep lovers cool on a hot night' called a **summer** bed. These beds each had four posts, with a common tester over an aisle.

Folding beds have always been a feature of the bed-joiner's art. The medieval **trussing** bed could be packed up for travelling, while the 18th-century designers produced ingenious beds that could be folded away and disguised as another piece of furniture. The **bureau bedstead** folded into a cupboard that resembled a desk; a **press bedstead** folded into a small press or chest of drawers, while with a **sofa bed,** a true 18th-century invention, the sofa opened out to make a bed.

By 1800, the necessity for heavy curtains and

hangings in the bedroom had gone, so leaving bare bedposts. By 1830 the posts had been cut down, and eventually disappeared into the head and foot boards. The **French bedstead** was introduced in the Regency. These *lit bateaux* were boat-shaped, with scroll ends with classical brass embellishments. They usually stood against the wall, with the flimsy hangings cascading down over the ends of the bed from a pole above. It was not until the Great Exhibition of 1851 that brass was used for bedsteads.

When beds, particularly those from the 18th century onwards, were very high off the ground, **bed-steps** were needed to climb up to the mattress. These often doubled as a close stool, with a chamber pot inside.

Babies' cots and cribs changed little in design over the centuries. Cradles were generally on rockers, an 18th-century refinement from Sheraton (qv) being one that was rocked by clockwork.

CERAMICS

INTRODUCTION

The art of fashioning pots and figurines from the earth is almost as old as man himself, and although the term 'ceramics' was only introduced in the 19th century, it derives from the ancient Greek word *keramos*, meaning pottery. It includes all articles made by firing clay, whether pottery or porcelain (qv). The working of this basic clay has no single origin, but evolved in a similar manner simultaneously at various places in the ancient world. Exactly how the clay was used depended then, as now, on its basic composition.

THE CRAFT

The earliest form of pottery, known as **pinch** or **squeeze** pottery, was simply made by pushing the thumb into a ball of moist clay and pulling up the sides. From this developed the **coil** method where a long 'sausage' of clay was rolled out and coiled round in a spiral to form the pot, each coil being pressed and smeared on to the one below. Both the inside and outside surfaces were then burnished with a polished stone or wooden bat to give a smooth finish. Forms of **moulding** were also used, particularly in ancient Greece.

Pots are known to have been made on a **potter's wheel** as early as the middle of the 3rd millennium BC. The basic method of 'throwing' a pot has altered little from the technique depicted in wall paintings in Egyptian tombs of c.1,900 BC save that their wheels were operated by a foot treadle or by hand, rather than by the electric power of today.

A ball of wet clay was placed in the centre of a circular, revolving tray or 'wheel', which was turned as fast as practical by hand or foot. The moist clay was then fashioned by expert hand, the sides drawn up into the required shape by the fingers. When partially dried the pot could be worked again, before glazing (qv) and firing (qv) in a fire or a kiln.

A later variation of the potter's wheel was that used for making hollow ware (such as bowls, cups and pots), by a technique called **jolleying**. Here the potter placed a ball of clay in a mould which was rotated on a wheel. A template was then lowered precisely on to the clay, so forcing it out to the sides of the mould and, at the same time, forming the inside of the vessel. The reverse is known as **jiggering**, which was mainly used for making flat-ware (plates and saucers). Here the inside of the piece was formed by the mould, the underside by the template. This was a far quicker method, but the results lacked the individuality of hand-thrown ware.

A very early and efficient method of creating ceramic pieces was by a process called **slip casting**. First, a highly porous mould was made of plaster of Paris. The slip (clay diluted with water to a creamy texture) was then poured into the mould. The water was absorbed from the slip into the plaster of Paris, leaving a deposit on the side of the mould. When the required thickness was achieved, the excess slip was poured away. As the slip dried out it contracted, and so the piece was easily removed from the mould. It was then cleaned up and fired. Slip casting was widely used from the early 18th century onwards for a great variety of pieces, particularly complicated figure models. The piece would be cast separately, then fused together using more slip before being fired.

FIRING

The process of firing clay is as old as the making of pottery itself. The most primitive form of firing pots was simply to bury them in a pit and light a fire on top. Kilns that could produce higher temperatures were known in the 4th millennium BC, and gradually advanced in design over the centuries.

The tunnel kilns of the 16th century were fired by wood – it was said that the foreman could tell when the temperature was right because his eyebrows began to singe! The bottle-shaped kilns used in the 18th and 19th century at the Staffordshire (qv) potteries were traditionally fired by coal, so making the pottery towns unhealthy under a pall of smoke. Today oil, gas and electricity have replaced coal as the energy source for kilns.

THE MATERIALS

Known chemically as hydrated silicate of aluminium, **clay** is the most common substance to come from decomposed feldspathic rock (granite or quartz). When powdered and mixed with water and sand, or other powdered rock, it can easily be shaped and moulded.

When the source of clay has not moved since the earth's formation, the clay is then in its purest form. Known as kaolin or china clay, this is only found in a few places in the world – China, where its properties were first discovered (hence the name china clay), Arita in Japan, parts of northern Europe (such as Limoges in France and Cornwall in England), the Ukraine, and parts of the United States (South Carolina and Ohio). This clay is the essential ingredient of **porcelain** (qv). Porcelain is distinct from pottery in that it is finer and remains white after firing.

POTTERY

Pottery is made from secondary clays, those that have been removed from their primary source by wind, rain or glacial action. Formed over millions of years, they are full of impurities and minerals, such as iron, which give the clay its red or brown colour after firing. There are five distinct kinds of pottery made from these secondary clays which, apart from the additives to the basic material, are only differentiated by the temperatures at which they are fired. They are earthenware, stoneware, saggar and fire clays, and terracotta.

Earthenware. Made from the 'common clay', earthenware pieces are fired at 950–1,100 degrees Fahrenheit. Temperatures of 700 degrees Fahrenheit were well within the means of primitive man, as pottery dating from the 6th millennium BC shows. One form of earthenware is **ironstone**, which is made extremely hard by the addition of glassy slag from iron ore smelting. Spode (qv) was the first to experiment with it c.1805, but it is chiefly associated with Miles Mason who patented the process in 1813, hence its more usual name of Mason's Ironstone. Because of its strength and cheapness it was widely used, and was decorated in every style.

Stoneware. With stoneware, the clays are generally more adaptable and easier to work with than earthenware, and are fired at 1,200–1,400 degrees Fahrenheit, which is hot enough to vitrify the rock additives, but not the clay. This makes the pottery very hard and non-porous, even when unglazed. The Chinese were making stoneware in the 4th century, but it was not known before the 9th century in Europe.

An unglazed red stoneware mug with relief decoration, mounted with a silver band round the lip. Staffordshire, c.1700

Saggar and fire clays. Both these sub-forms of stoneware were designed to withstand great heat. Saggar clay was named after its principal use, that of separating other ceramic pieces being fired in the kiln. Fire clays were used for kiln linings and fire bricks.

Terracotta. Terracotta clays are generally fired at a very low temperature and are unglazed and therefore porous. They are reddish in colour and most commonly used for sculpture, garden pots and secondary building materials.

PORCELAIN

In the early 17th century, Portuguese traders brought back from China a type of earthenware with a fine, semi-transparent texture which eventually became known as **porcelain**. A charming, but probably inaccurate suggestion for the origin of the term is that it comes from *porcellana,* the Portuguese word for a cowrie shell, whose polished underside resembles porcelain and whose back looks like a little pig. This Oriental porcelain, however, was known throughout the East by its Persian name, *cheny,* the same word they used for its country of origin, China. Until the 19th century in England, porcelain was also known as china, pronounced in the Persian way 'cheenee'.

Oriental hard-paste porcelain. True porcelain or, as it became known, hard-paste porcelain, was made in China from the 7th or 8th century onwards from the primary clay, kaolin, to hold the form when fired, combined with china stone, a white feldspar rock called 'petunse', to give it its natural glaze. Thus the piece could be fired and glazed at the same time. An alternative was to fire the piece at a lower temperature (known as biscuit firing), then refire it at a higher temperature once the glaze or decoration had been applied.

The Japanese, too, had discovered the secret of making porcelain when in the early 17th century a source of china clay was discovered at Arita. The pieces were shipped from the port of Imari, hence their name, **Imari** ware. They were generally lavishly decorated with flowers or ships, in rich, deep colours of blue, red and gold, also aubergine, turquoise and green. When copied by the Chinese, it was known as **Chinese Imari** ware. In the 18th and 19th century some of the designs, such as the 'Brocaded Imari' after

A Chinese blue-and-white vase, 16th century

a floral brocade silk textile, were reproduced in England by the Derby, Worcester and Spode factories.

Soft-paste porcelain. As the secret of fine porcelain manufacture was understandably well guarded by the Chinese and Japanese, the Europeans had to resort to finding their own substitute for the porcelain they admired so much. Although the Persians were making a passable substitute in the late 11th and early 12th century, it was not until the end of the 16th century that something approaching porcelain was achieved in the Medici factories in Florence. True porcelain is translucent when held up to the light, and the only material known with similar properties was glass. After much trial and error, the correct mixture of white clay and powdered glass was fused together to make what was called soft-paste porcelain. The firing temperature, c.1,200 degrees Fahrenheit, was critical. This technique spread at the end of the 17th century to many notable factories in France (including Sèvres), and much later to England, where it was employed by such factories as Chelsea, Bow, Derby and Worcester.

A further refinement, the addition of bone ash to the soft-paste porcelain to make **bone china**, was made at the Bow factory (qv) in the 1750s, and further developed by Josiah Spode (qv) in the early 1800s. Its appeal was threefold: it was cheap to produce, more durable, and it was much more reliable during the firing process. Bone china is made in England today in great quantities.

Another development in the 18th century was **soaprock porcelain**. Here the soft soaprock or soapstone, a form of magnesium silicate, was used as a substitute for feldspar. The practice was first introduced in Bristol, and spread to other factories, notably Worcester (qv) who took over the Bristol factory.

European hard-paste porcelain. At the beginning of the 18th century an alchemist called Johann Böttger was working for Augustus the Strong of Saxony (so named for his 350 children). When his quest to make gold from a base metal failed, his talents were forcibly redirected towards discovering the Chinese secret of making hard-paste porcelain. In 1708 he succeeded, and two years later, the Royal Saxon Porcelain Manufacture was established at Meissen. Their secret was not safe for long, as two workers defected, first to Austria and then to Venice. However, the secret of hard-paste porcelain was discovered quite independently in England by a Quaker apothecary, William Cookworthy of Plymouth. He found a source of china clay and china stone on Lord Camelford's estate near Truro in Cornwall. Unfortunately, by the time he had patented his discovery in 1768 imported Chinese blue-and-white porcelain had become relatively cheap.

THE DECORATION

One of the earliest forms of pottery decoration developed from practicality. The early potter discovered that by coating a vessel with a **slip coat**, a watered-down version of the clay and firing it, it would become non-porous. The addition of a slip coat also made decoration easier to apply, either by adding a colour or by scratching a design through to the base. Both the Greeks and Romans produced marvellous examples of this decoration. Alternatively, layers of slip decoration, applied from a bag and squeezed through a nozzle (like icing a cake), could be built up in relief. Slip coating in England reached its height in the 17th and early 18th century, the names of Thomas and Ralph Toft being foremost among the makers in Staffordshire (qv). The design, usually a primitive picture or Puritan religious saying, was quite crudely worked.

When slip decoration is applied to porcelain it is known as *pâte-sur-pâte* – paste on paste. The slip coat is built up in many layers over a biscuit (unglazed) base and then carved in relief. The method was used first in China in the 18th century, and then in France at Sèvres, and in England at Minton (qv) during the 19th century.

GLAZES

The use of a **glaze** is another common form of finishing pottery and porcelain to make it serviceable or decorative, or both. As early as 1,700 BC, the Egyptians were using powdered glass, soda, or other alkaline compounds to glaze their pottery. The addition of copper to the glaze turned it a wondrous blue, or turquoise. These glazes, however, tended to craze and peel, and it was found that the addition of galena, a lead sulphide, fixed the glaze permanently. **Lead** glazes were used extensively from the Middle Ages onwards in England. Their formula comprised sand, salt and an alkali such as potash, fused with lead oxide. The fired pottery was painted with, or dipped, into the glaze, and re-fired at a lower temperature. The resultant glaze was totally transparent. Because of the extreme toxicity of the lead, these glazes were abandoned in the early 19th century.

A form of **tin** glaze was being used to decorate bricks on houses in Babylon in the 4th century, but the process was lost until the Persians rediscovered it in the 8th century. The art of tin glazing earthenware (made from lead and tin oxide, combined with silicate of potash which gives a white glaze) spread first to Spain with the Moors, then to the rest of Europe. It came to Italy from the Balearic island of Majorca, hence its Italian name, **maiolica**. It was known as **faience** in France, Spain and Germany. By 1584 it was being made in England and in Holland, where it was established in the town of Delft. **Delftware** with a capital D is Dutch, whereas 'delftware' with a small d is English. Early in the 17th century, the Dutch East India Company imported quantities of Chinese porcelain decorated in blue on a white background. These designs and styles, known as 'blue-and-white', were copied on to delftware with great success for those who could not afford Chinese porcelain. Some factories worked out of disused breweries, and took their names, such as The Moor's Head. Prodigious quantities of pottery were produced – dinner services, vases, even *tulipières* (tall pagoda-shaped vases for holding tulips) and tiles.

The Rhinelanders are credited with the invention of the **salt** glaze in the 14th century. It was mainly used for drinking vessels, such as the one known as a 'Bellarmine' or greybeard, decorated on the neck with the bearded caricature of the unpopular Cardinal Bellarmine. Stoneware pieces were fired in the normal way and, when the kiln was at its maximum heat, a quantity of salt (sodium chloride) was thrown into the kiln. The heat vapourized the salt so that the chloride evaporated through the chimney, while the sodium

A plate of blue-painted delftware. Bristol, c.1730

combined with the silicates in the stoneware to form a thin salt glaze. It is easily recognized by its texture of orange peel. Salt glaze stoneware was introduced to England in 1671 when John Dwight, a Fulham potter, was granted the patent by Charles II for 'the Misterie of The Stone Ware vulgarly called Cologne Ware'. Stoneware is a very versatile medium, equally suited to the early busts created by John Dwight and to the water pipes and drains of today.

The process of creating **lustre ware**, the decorative deposit of a metal on pottery, was discovered by the glass painters of Egypt in the 7th century BC, and later refined by the potters of Baghdad. Metallic oxides, such as silver or copper, were applied to the glazed surface and fired at a relatively low temperature. Lustre was difficult to achieve by this process, and a simpler form was eventually developed by the Staffordshire potters in the 18th century. Gold provided a coppery pink or purple lustre, copper produced a yellowy to deep coppery red, while silver gave a yellowy straw colour. Occasionally a piece such as a tea or coffee pot would be entirely covered with lustre to emulate silver. **Resist lustre** was a form of decoration where wax, varnish or a paper stencil was applied to the piece before firing so that it would resist the lustre. With 'splash lustre', oil was splashed on to copper lustre before firing, to give a speckled effect. Rather crude lustreware was made in many factories during the 19th century, and is often termed Sunderland ware after one of them. Later copies abound.

When porcelain was left unglazed, it was known as **biscuit porcelain** (sometimes termed as *bisque*), and was widely used for figures, especially classical statues, in the 18th century. As any blemish in the porcelain could not be disguised with a later glaze or painting, it was correspondingly more expensive. A cheaper version, developed at the Copeland factory in the mid-19th century, was called **Parian ware,** or 'statuary porcelain'. It can be finely moulded and, as it closely resembles a very pure, white marble, it was commonly used for statues.

PAINTING AND PRINTING

During the 14th century it was discovered that the pigment cobalt, imported from Persia, could withstand the high temperatures required for firing glazed pottery. This deep blue was used for both the ground and, more usually, the decoration. As this decoration was close to the admired Chinese porcelain, it too became known as 'blue-and-white' and the designs were greatly influenced by the Chinese style. Blue-and-white could also be decorated on top of the glaze after firing with enamels.

The paints used by the porcelain artists were finely ground metallic oxide pigments, mixed with oil derived from the residue of evaporated turpentine and, to keep this creamy paste workable, aniseed oil. The Chinese had perfected the art of painting with enamels, a skill that came to London via Paris in the early 18th century.

The art of painting on porcelain required immense skill. The decoration was painted directly on to the glazed surface, but as only colours that matured at the same temperature could be fired together, only those colours could be applied at the same time. Thus, depending on the number of colours, the piece might have to be fired as many as five times. Furthermore,

A jug with painted relief decoration, c.1845

the artist also had to take into account that the colours changed shades during firing.

The art of **transfer printing** on ceramics was developed in the mid-18th century at Doccia in Italy, and perfected by the British through decorating enamel boxes. A copper plate was either engraved or etched, sometimes a combination of the two, with the chosen design. A thin film of blue or black ink was applied to the engraved plate, and a sheet of tissue paper was laid on top. The paper bearing the image was then transferred to the glazed piece to be decorated, firmed down, then removed. The image was then fixed by firing as it sank into the glaze. Often the transfer sheets overlapped, leaving lines in the decoration. The **Willow Pattern**, first produced by the Caughley factory in 1780, was made in prodigious quantities by this method in over 200 English factories – so popular was it that it was even copied by the Chinese. Although set in China, the story of the Willow Pattern is English. A mandarin has promised his daughter in marriage to a rich old merchant, but she is in love with another. Their secret meetings are discovered, and she is locked in her room within the pagoda, set in a walled garden. On the morning of the marriage, she escapes and elopes with her lover. They are chased by her father across the bridge as they head for the boat. To escape capture, they are transformed into doves.

A refinement of transfer printing was **bat printing** where the stipple-engraved design was applied to a 'bat' of glue instead of paper. The result was far softer. Stipple engraving was also employed to make colour transfers, usually on pot lids in the early 19th century. These pieces are now known as **Pratt ware** after Felix Pratt, a Staffordshire potter who, among many others, used this method of decoration.

GILDING AND OTHER METHODS

Gilding was the ultimate decoration for all ceramics. Early attempts at cold gilding, where gold leaf was applied with a size, were unsuccessful as it invariably rubbed off with use. A more successful form used in the early 18th century was called **honey gilding**. Here, gold leaf was mixed with honey which was then melted away with boiling water. The resulting gold powder was applied to the glazed surface with a 'vinaigrette' of garlic oil and vinegar mixed with gum water, and then fired. The result was a rich, but somewhat dull, brown gold. The **mercury gilding** of the late 18th century, where the gold was dissolved in mercury, gave a far brighter, more durable and lasting finish. The amalgam was painted on to the glazed surface and during the firing the mercury was driven off in a cloud of noxious fumes, leaving a gold film. This was then burnished, often by the wife of the gilder, by skilful use of the 'burnishing tool', usually a smooth agate (dogs' teeth were also used) mounted on a wooden handle. For a dull surface, a rougher mounted agate was used. Often, the two were used in conjunction to produce intricate patterns within the gilding.

Another common form of decoration from the 18th century onwards was **reticulation**, named after a 'reticule', a network bag made of string which the effect resembled. The finished piece, often a plate or a vase, was dried out to 'leather hardness', before small pieces of clay were cut out with a sharp knife in the chosen pattern. This could be a diamond network on the edge of a plate to resemble an intertwined ribbon, or a pattern of holes over an entire vase. The piece was then glazed and fired. One form of decoration first used by the Chinese and Japanese in the 17th century was **rice grain** decoration. Small perforations were made in the clay in the shape of grains of rice, and these then filled with glaze.

THE FACTORIES

THE MAJOR FACTORIES

Chelsea. The earliest English porcelain was made at the Chelsea works, founded in about 1745 by a silversmith, Nicholas Sprimont, and a jeweller, Charles Gouyn, both of Huguenot descent. The factory made soft-paste porcelain whose styles developed during four distinctive periods, defined by separate marks. The shapes of much of the early work (1745–49) bear an 'incised triangle' mark, and were inspired by the current rococo fashion in silver, such as shells and acanthus leaves. The decoration was relatively plain, with the minimum of painted decoration to cover blemishes. Pieces made between 1749 and 1752 had a 'raised anchor' mark (an anchor on a medallion cast in relief), and were often decorated with flowers, landscapes and scenes from Aesop's Fables, or with oriental designs. The 'red anchor' period (1752–58) is considered the finest, producing tureens and dishes in the shapes of birds, animals and vegetables, some superb figures, 'Chelsea toys', tiny scent bottles and patch boxes. The 'gold anchor' period (1758–70) is marked by an ever-increasing sumptuousness and sophistication, with deep backgrounds of royal or

A porcelain scent bottle in the form of a lady dancing, mounted in gold. Chelsea, c.1755

'Mazzarin' blue, pea green or claret, all with lavish gilding inspired by French Sèvres porcelain. Brightly painted figures stood before elaborate bocages (thickets covered in flowers), and rococo scrolls and exotic painted birds abounded. The factory was sold in 1770 to William Duesbury and John Heath, both of Derby (qv). The combined mark of the gold anchor intertwined with the letter 'D', was used until the factory was finally closed in 1784.

Derby. André Planché was making soft-paste porcelain figures in Derby in the 1750s, but the main Derby factory had been set up by William Duesbury and John Heath by 1756. It produced a wide variety of porcelain, the early work characteristically rather heavy and creamy-white in colour, such as the Chinese figure groups, boars and goats. Some pieces were unsuccessful copies of Chelsea ware, even with a faithful reproduction of their gold anchor mark. In 1770 Duesbury bought the defunct Chelsea factory.

The next phase of Derby was characterized by stiffly posed figures in pale, delicate colours. Heavy blue-tone glazes were also used in an attempt to emulate the hard-paste porcelains of the Continent, so much so that they advertised their factory as 'the second Dresden'. Derby tableware, however, was well painted, particularly the landscapes, bird and botanical subjects. Moths were not an uncommon subject. William Duesbury died in 1786 and was succeeded by his son, who himself died in 1796. This later period is marked by the finely modelled biscuit figures with their fine detail of simulated marble in the neo-classical style. In 1811 the factory was sold to Robert Bloor, who ran it until 1826 when he was certified insane. This period is marked by pieces decorated in the showy 'Japan style', lavish decoration with heavy gilding, and by the reissue of figures made from earlier moulds. The factory was run by James Thomason and Thomas Clarke until its closure in 1848. A new company was formed in 1876 and was appointed 'Manufacturers of Porcelain to Her Majesty' (Queen Victoria), hence its present name Royal Crown Derby.

Bow. The Bow factory was established during the 1740s in Stratford, south-east London, on the north side of Bow Bridge. According to the patent of the founder, Thomas Frye, it produced pieces of a 'certain material equal in beauty to imported porcelain, from a recipe including a material called unaker, the produce of the Cherokee nation of America'. Later patents were taken out for porcelain that included bone-ash, known as 'Virgin Earth', which produced pieces that were contemporarily described as 'little inferior to those which were brought from China', hence the name for their works, 'New Canton'. Early Bow porcelain figures, such as the muses or women with children, were made from a creamy bone-paste and were either plain white or sparsely painted, while the useful ware was frequently decorated in the Chinese or Japanese manner. Later pieces of the 1750s had a waxy, blue underglaze with bright, clear colouring to the delicate painting. During the final period, until the factory's closure in 1776, the figures tended to become heavier with extravagant, richly enamelled decoration, often with a bocage full of flowers.

Lowestoft. The Lowestoft factory in Suffolk began making fine quality soft-paste porcelain, similar in style and composition to that from Bow, in 1757. It specialized in tableware and tea services, often painted in the Chinese style, and is characterized by the use of a blue underglaze. The Lowestoft Works were well known for their wares celebrating special events, and for 'trifle' pieces, inexpensive gifts made for the visitors' market. The factory closed in 1802.

Worcester. The Royal Worcester Porcelain Company of today can trace an unbroken history back to 1751. In 1752 the Worcester factory took over the one at Bristol, adopting their soapstone soft-paste porcelain and employing many of their workers. The distinctive early Worcester style soon developed, in the Chinese fashion of the blue underglaze, or landscapes on yellow backgrounds, polychrome flower sprays, fantastic birds, figure subjects (often in a soft purple monochrome), and black transfer printing. The

Japanese brocaded Imari design was used until 1775. Redundant Chelsea painters also took their skills and elaborate Sèvres-style decoration to Worcester and from 1770 onwards the scale blue (a deep, blackish blue) background with panels for exotic birds, flowers and figure subjects were standard Worcester decoration. Worcester followed the prevailing fashion, particularly the neo-classical designs of the 1780s, of swags and urns.

In 1783, the factory was bought by Thomas Flight for his sons Joseph and John, and renamed 'Flight Worcester'. At the end of the 18th century the decoration was of great importance – landscapes, shells, feathers and portraits executed in greys, sepia or colour are all typical of the Worcester production faithfully following the neo-classical trend. Seaweed and the wavy *vermicule* (literally 'worm') were also typical backgrounds often richly gilded as well. In 1792, on the death of John Flight, Martin Barr joined the firm which then became 'Flight and Barr'. It was

A stemmed bowl
of reticulated porcelain. Worcester, late 1840s

called variously 'Barr, Flight and Barr' (1807–13) and 'Flight, Barr and Barr', until in 1840 it was amalgamated with the factory set up by a former Worcester director, Robert Chamberlain. From 1862 it was known as the Royal Worcester Porcelain Company. Typical of Worcester in the 19th century were the figures in Parian ware (qv), styles emulating Japanese Satsuma ware and the rich dinner services inspired by Sèvres and other continental factories.

Caughley. This Shropshire factory was founded in 1750 to manufacture earthenware, but in 1772 ownership passed to Thomas Turner who began producing soft-paste porcelain. Turner had worked at Worcester, as had his associate Robert Hancock, with the result that Caughley porcelain closely resembles Worcester in body (the use of soapstone), style and decoration, particularly the transfer printing in blue underglaze. The Willow Pattern and the Broseley Blue Dragon, both in use today, were both said to be the work of Thomas Minton, an engraver working for Turner at that time. Flower sprigs and gilding, particularly with blue-and-white wares, is another characteristic of Caughley porcelain. In 1799, the factory was sold to John Rose of Coalport, a former apprentice to Turner.

Coalport. John Rose founded his Coalport factory in Shropshire in 1796 and after the acquisition of Caughley operated the two together until 1814. Pieces from the two factories were therefore naturally similar in design and decoration. The famous Indian Tree pattern was introduced in 1801, and widely copied by other factories in later years. In 1819 Rose employed William Billingsley, a fine painter who had worked at Derby, who brought not only his painting skill, but the moulds and white porcelain stock of the two defunct Welsh factories of Swansea and Nantgarw. The porcelain now had a remarkable translucency. Rose was awarded the Gold Medal by the Royal Society of Arts in 1820 for his development of a feldspathic glaze that replaced the highly toxic lead glaze. Although vases covered with modelled flowers and highly painted dessert services are characteristic of Coalport, copies of Sèvres and the Chelsea gold anchor period were also produced. The factory was reorganized in 1885 as the Coalport China Company.

New Hall. The New Hall factory at Sheldon in Staffordshire was founded in 1781, after a consortium of six Staffordshire potters bought the patent for hard-paste porcelain from Richard Champion of Bristol (who in turn had bought it from the originator, Cookworthy (qv)). The early New Hall shows a strong Chinese influence in style and decorating, copied from Chinese export pieces. Floral sprays are also common on their 'useful ware' – tea services, jugs and dessert services. From about 1810 a softer bone china was produced, much of it bat-printed. The factory closed in 1835.

Rockingham. A pottery factory, founded in c.1745 on the Marquis of Rockingham's estate at Swinton in Yorkshire, began by making brown and white stoneware. In 1778 John and William Brameld with Thomas Bingley took over the factory and began making earthenware. From c.1806 the factory developed a purple-brown glaze, from manganese oxide, which became known as Rockingham glaze. One famous Rockingham piece was the **Cadogan teapot** modelled on a 17th century Chinese porcelain wine pot that had no lid as it was filled through a cone-like opening in the base. When the peach-shaped pot was turned over, the tea (supposedly) did not spill. It was named after the Honourable Mrs Cadogan, who brought the Chinese original to England and had it copied. The factory floundered after bad debts from Russia, but was saved in 1826 by the 5th Earl Fitzwilliam (grandson of the last Marquis of Rockingham). From that time, the factory changed to the production of porcelain and took the Rockingham crest, a griffin, as its mark. Their style was based on Coalport (so much so that dealers joke that 'when you buy it it's Coalport, when you sell it it's Rockingham'!). The factory closed in 1842.

Spode. The introduction of bone china to the Staffordshire potteries is credited to Josiah Spode II, son of the founder of the Spode factory of the same name. Spode senior opened the factory in 1770, and was the first to decorate his pearlware with underglaze blue transfer prints, which were usually marked 'Spode' in the same blue. His work in this medium greatly improved the quality of transfer printing, so much so that attractive tableware could be made comparatively inexpensively. Spode also produced stone china, a hard, white earthenware containing china-stone that made a cheap substitute for porcelain. The rights for this were probably bought from Turner (qv). Josiah Spode II was joined in 1813 by W. T. Copeland and the firm was named Spode & Copeland. On the death of Josiah Spode III in 1829 Copeland bought the firm, which since 1847 has been called W. T. Copeland & Son. The earlier works are of the Empire style with new ground colours of turquoise, vermilion and Sardinian green. Both transfer- and bat-printed pieces were typical for tea and dinner services, as were Japanese patterns.

Minton. Thomas Minton's name is first connected with Caughley (qv), where he produced the Willow and the Blue Dragon patterns before he founded his own factory in 1793 at Stoke-on-Trent, Staffordshire. Not surprisingly, his early work was mostly in printed patterns in underglaze blue, made primarily for the burgeoning American market. Manufacturing soft-paste porcelain until 1811, the factory transferred to bone china in 1821, producing marvellous copies of Sèvres, Meissen and Chelsea ware all of excellent workmanship and quality. By the mid-19th century, it was renowned for its maiolica (qv) and Parian ware (qv). Minton's forte in the late 19th century, *pâte-sur-pâte* (qv), was particularly fine. The factory passed through several owners, and since 1883 has been called Minton's Ltd.

THE MAJOR ENGLISH POTTERIES

Astbury. The potter John Astbury (1686–1743) and his son Thomas were the originators of Astbury-type ware, a form of pottery made in in red clay decorated with white clay under a transparent lead glaze. The Astburys were also credited with the introduction of calcinated and ground flint into their pottery, which gave it a whiter and finer texture, and for their models of fairly primitive mounted horses and soldiers, teapots and jugs. Mottled pieces are termed Astbury-Whieldon ware after Thomas Whieldon who developed a glaze with metallic oxides that produced a 'splashed' effect.

Wood. Of the large Staffordshire family of potters in Burslem, Ralph Wood (1715–72), maker of finely modelled figures, is probably the best known. These pieces were covered in such sophisticated lead glazes, yellow, purplish-brown, green and grey, that they resembled enamels. Wood first introduced the Toby Jug modelled on a man holding a tankard of beer in one hand and a pipe in the other. The name came from Toby Philpot, a character in a song called 'The Brown Jug'. A variation, 'The Night Watchman', depicts a man seated with a lantern, with a woman, Martha Gunn, a bathing hut attendant from Brighton. Ralph Wood's nephew, Enoch Wood, was for a time in partnership with Ralph Wood II, who continued the family tradition of producing figures as well as underglaze blue printed wares, particularly for the American market.

Wedgwood. No single man has made a greater contribution to British ceramics than Josiah Wedgwood (1730–95). He was the twelfth son of a fourth generation potter from Burslem, Staffordshire. Apprenticed to his brother Thomas, he developed his skills as a potter before joining Thomas Whieldon (qv) in 1754. There he experimented with both the composition of earthenware and its glazes.

In 1759 Wedgwood set up on his own at the Ivy House Works, where he continued to experiment, producing a fine, green semi-translucent glaze. Up to that time, most earthenware was of a practical, or as it was termed, a 'useful', nature. Wedgwood changed that practice by making these useful pieces decorative as well. His **cauliflower ware**, modelled in the shape of the vegetable, was used for teapots, jugs and bowls for which his new glaze was well suited. His greatest breakthrough, however, came in 1763, when he perfected an earthenware called **creamware**, also known as ivoryware. The light and creamy-white body, achieved by the addition of ground flint and pipe clay under a silky lead glaze, superseded delft (qv) and salt-glaze (qv) stoneware both in England and on the Continent. The name was changed to **Queen's ware** after an order for a tea service in 1762 from Queen Charlotte. Another notable client was Catherine the Great of Russia who ordered a complete dinner service for 50 people, comprising 952 pieces, all hand-painted with English 'wild and romantic' scenes. Destined for her Grenouillère Palace in St Petersburg, it was known as the 'Frog Service'. Creamware was extremely versatile with dozens of domestic uses – dinner services, table centrepieces, candlesticks, inkwells and a host of other wares. It could be left plain, or decorated by painting or transfer printing. It was also inexpensive to produce. Creamware was made by many factories in England, particularly in Leeds and Liverpool, and throughout Europe and the Americas when the secret formula was discovered. In France it was made at Luneville and called *terre du pipe* (pipe clay), and in Italy *terraglia inglese.* A further refinement of Queen's ware made by Wedgwood in the 1780s was **pearl ware**. The larger proportion of flint and white clay and the small addition of cobalt to the lead glaze made it whiter in appearance and gave it the milky iridescence of real pearls.

With great vision, Wedgwood saw that his earthenware could be turned to the prevailing neo-classical style. In 1769 he took Thomas Bentley as a partner and opened the Etruria factory purely for ornamental work. This period, until Bentley's death in 1780, produced the factory's finest pieces. They experimented with a form of stoneware known as

Egyptian Black, which Wedgwood called **black basalt**. His basaltes, made from Staffordshire clay, ironstone slag and manganese oxide, were far finer and infinitely harder than anything previously known. It took a deep polish and, being so hard and fine, it resembled porcelain. Often, it was further decorated with enamel colours. Black basaltes were used for vases, sometimes very large busts, particularly those of philosophers and writers to decorate libraries, and medallions. **Rosso antico**, a dark red stoneware, was used for similar purposes, particularly when decorated with black figures in imitation of ancient Greek vases.

Although Wedgwood referred to his basaltes as 'black porcelain', the **jasper ware** he developed in 1774 was named 'biscuit porcelain' as, being white and semi-translucent when thinly cast, it did resemble porcelain. The essential ingredient of this fine, close-grained stoneware was barium sulphate (called 'cawk' by Wedgwood), and, being 'biscuit ware' it was always left unglazed. Jasper ware could be successfully stained with metallic oxides – lilac, yellow, maroon, sage green, black and the ubiquitous 'Wedgwood blue', a soft, pale blue, as well as a darker blue. This coloured, matt finish was a splendid background for applied classical relief decorations and portraits, and was used extensively on vases, plaques, friezes (particularly those commissioned by the Adam brothers (qv)) and cameos, even sword hilts. Many of these neo-classical pieces are still being made today.

The most famous piece of jasper ware is Wedgwood's reproduction of the Portland Vase. The original vase of the 1st century AD was made of cased glass with white relief, and was found in a Roman sarcophagus. It was owned by the Barberini family in the 17th century, and, in about 1780, it was sold to a Scottish dealer, who passed it on to Sir William Hamilton. He brought it back to London, where a great collector of the day, 'a sober lady but much intoxicated by empty vases', the Dowager Duchess of Portland, acquired it. On her death it was auctioned and bought by her grandson, the 3rd Duke. He lent it to Wedgwood, who made 16 copies of it in jasper, before it was sent to the British Museum where it

JOSIAH WEDGWOOD
Feb. 2nd 1805

wedgwood WEDGWOOD

The marks used by the Wedgwood factory

went on permanent loan. In 1845 a drunken, disaffected museum employee smashed the vase into over a hundred pieces. It was repaired and put on show. In 1945 the museum finally bought the vase and repaired it to better effect. Other ancient vases from Sir William Hamilton's collection were copied by the score by Wedgwood and decorated in his studio in Chelsea.

Another development pioneered by Wedgwood and much copied by other Staffordshire potteries was **cane ware**, so called from its light buff colour and its frequent use as simulated bamboo. Dishes made of cane ware were known as 'ceramic pastry', as they replaced real pie-crust pastry when flour became scarce during the Napoleonic Wars.

Josiah Wedgwood died in 1795 and was succeeded by his third son, also Josiah. He began the manufacture of bone china in 1812 when Queen's ware went out of fashion but he allowed the factory to run into serious financial difficulties, from which it did not recover until the end of the 19th century. During these years it generally followed fashion, producing maiolica (qv), and Parian ware (qv), which it termed 'Carrara'. The factory is still producing their fine range of wares today.

THE MARKS

All the important ceramic factories used marks and numbers so that the retailer could identify the exact provenance, style and batch of each piece for re-ordering. This legacy has greatly simplified the identification of ceramics in later years and made forgery more difficult. Marks that purport to pre-date 1840 should, however, be viewed with care.

The most important development in ceramic marking was the McKinley Tariff Act, passed by the Americans in 1891 as the result of trading conflicts between the United States and Europe. This stated that articles imported into the United States must have the country of origin clearly marked, so that the tariff applicable for each country could be correctly charged. Thus, if the word **ENGLAND** forms part of the mark the piece is likely to be post-1891. **Made in England** or **Bone China** indicates 20th-century manufacture.

The words **Trade Mark** in a ceramic mark mean that the piece is post-1862, the year of the Trade Mark Act. The word **Limited** or Ltd. is found after 1861. The inclusion of the word **Royal** in a factory mark is unlikely to date from earlier than 1850. If the **Royal arms** are printed, the piece may be 19th century, but is more likely to be modern. When the name of the

pattern, for example Indian Tree, is printed in the mark the piece is post-1810. When a diamond-shaped motif, surrounding the abbreviation **Rd No**, letters and numbers, is incised on the bottom, the piece can be accurately dated between 1842 and 1883. This is a design registration mark, whose numbers refer to the shape or pattern registered with the Patent Office.

GLASS

INTRODUCTION

Glass is the most remarkable substance, made from the simplest and cheapest of materials. It can be transparent, translucent or opaque, coloured or colourless. It can be moulded or formed into an infinite variety of shapes. Plain, or with decoration, it can be very beautiful. Being both readily cleaned and impermeable to liquids, glass is functional, and has been used for centuries for eating and drinking from. Its optical properties are a science on their own. Glass can also be melted down and reused. Like many crafts, the basic materials and methods of working have altered little over thousands of years.

THE CRAFT

BLOWING AND MOULDING

A rudimentary form of glass (beads and seals), probably discovered by accident during the smelting of metals, was known in Syria in the 3rd millennium BC. Early glass vessels from Syria and Egypt, made during the 2nd millennium BC were formed by pouring molten glass in a spiral over a rod or mould. By the 1st century BC techniques had been considerably advanced by the Romans, who discovered how to work molten glass with a blow-pipe (qv). They also perfected the first 'mass-produced' glassware by blowing molten glass into a mould, so making identical pieces. The art of glass making spread throughout the Roman colonies. By the fall of the Roman Empire in the 5th century AD, the craft was sufficiently well established on the banks of the Rhône and the Seine not to die out completely in the Dark Ages.

As the Venetians had close trading links with Syria

during the 15th century they were able to import the fine Syrian ash (qv) and Egyptian soda for making their superior glass. The threat of fire from the glass factories sited throughout the city forced the glass-makers to move to the nearby island of Murano, where they remain to this day. From here glass making spread throughout Europe (where ash from burnt wood, mostly beech, straw, hay and bracken was used as an alkali), and thence to England. Dyers Cross in the Weald of Kent and Chiddingfold in Surrey became the main centres of glass making, so much so that on a Venetian tapestry map of Europe dated 1540, the only place marked in England is Chiddingfold.

The glass-maker's basic tools have altered little since the 1st century BC. They are a simple blow-pipe, a pontil or iron rod, tongs, wooden paddles and moulds, shears, and a marver, a flat slab of marble or stone on which to shape the pieces.

The most common item of blown glass was, and still is, the wine glass. A gather, or blob of molten glass, was picked up at the end of the blow-pipe and blown by the glass-maker into a bubble. The tube was then rotated, the stem of the glass being drawn out from the bottom of the bubble by the pontil. The foot was formed by allowing a new gather to run off the end of the pontil on to the marver. The stalk was cut off with the shears and the round blob of glass attached to the stem. The foot was then worked into shape by the paddles and tongs, the whole being constantly rotated on the end of the blow-pipe and reheated. The blow-pipe was then cracked off the top of the bubble after the base of the glass had been attached to the pontil at the centre of the foot. The top was then reheated, and the rim trimmed with the shears. The final shaping, both inside and out, was done with the tongs. The pontil was broken off, the scar being called a 'pontil mark'. These were either ground off or not, depending on the quality of the glass and the date of manufacture – after 1800 the pontil mark was always removed, although this alone is no clue to age. In the late 18th century, glasses were formed separately in three stages, the bowl, the stem and the foot.

A glass beaker of a mould-blown design and thread foot, c.1600

The Romans perfected the art of forming glass artefacts by **mould-blowing**, achieved by blowing molten glass into a mould. The process was refined and became widespread in the early 19th century with the development of a flint glass that, although inferior in quality, solidified quickly in the mould. Mould-blown glass could be cut with a wheel, but the results were never as good as with blown glass.

Blown, moulded glass was mechanized in 1825. The process, patented by an American named Bakewell, was called **press-moulding**. The mould formed the outside shape and decoration, while the plunger that rammed the molten gather into the mould was in the shape of the inside of the piece. One American manufacturer was the Sandwich Glass Company, hence pressed glass being often known as 'Sandwich Glass'. Press-moulding came to England in the 1830s. The early machines were hand-operated, but by 1864 steam presses were introduced. Although this process could produce pieces to emulate cut glass, they never had the brilliance or quality of the real thing.

FLAT GLASS

The making of flat glass for window panes and mirrors was ably described by the German monk Theophilus in his *Diversarum Artium Schedula*, written AD c.1000. By a technique known as the **broad process**, a very long bubble of glass was blown and, while still malleable, its top and bottom were cut off. The resulting tube was cut open and flattened out. After it had cooled, it was ground and polished by hand. The result was not always wholly satisfactory, as the glass was uneven in both texture and colour.

An even earlier flat glass, developed by the Syrians for windows, was called **crown glass**. This was made by spinning a large molten blob of gather on a rod, the centrifugal force forming the glass into a wide, thin, flat disc. This was then cut into the required shapes, such as diamonds for leaded windows. The bulbous centre piece, called the 'bullion point', often to be seen in old window panes is now much copied.

Towards the end of the 17th century the French were casting glass in sheets, which they exported to Britain. Here, molten glass was poured into an iron box, and run off into a tray. The slowly cooling glass was then rolled flat with a cast iron roller. When absolutely cool, the sheet of glass was polished by rubbing two pieces together with a powder between them. The lower sheet was held in putty, the upper was under tension from above. **Bevelling** was done by hand, but, at the end of the 17th century an 'engine for Grinding, Polishing, and Cutting Looking-Glass Plates' was already in use. The British Cast Plate-Glass Company at St Helens, Lancashire, began casting glass in England at the end of the 18th century.

SILVERING

In 1500 the glass manufacturers of Murano near Venice held the monopoly in making mirrors. The process finally reached England in the early 17th century, when Sir Robert Mansell imported 'many expert strangers from foreign parts beyond the seas' to work in his factory in Lambeth, London. Soon after the Restoration, the Duke of Buckingham set up his famous mirror works at the Glass House, Vauxhall – hence old mirrored glass made by the broad process was contemporarily known as Vauxhall glass.

The term silvering is deceptive, for although a small quantity of silver is used in mirrored glass today, none was used in the early process. Until the mid-19th century glass was mirrored by a process known as **foiling**, or foliating. A sheet of blotting paper sprinkled with chalk was laid on a smooth, flat surface. A wafer-thin sheet of tin foil was placed over this, then a thick film of mercury was spread over the foil, using a hare's foot. A sheet of paper was then laid on top and finally the sheet of glass. The paper was then carefully pulled out, leaving the amalgam of tin and mercury to adhere evenly to the glass. The glass was weighted and the excess mercury squeezed out. As this process could only be used for flat glass, convex and concave mirrors were silvered with a mixture of mercury, tin, lead and bismuth. The molten liquid was simply painted on to the glass. Both these methods were superseded by the invention in 1840 of a chemical process of silvering glass that was far safer than using mercury and, for the first time, did actually contain silver.

To check the age of a mirror, place a pencil with a sharp point against the glass. The closer the image to the lead of the pencil, the older the mirror. Modern glass has a greenish tinge, and gives a substantial image; old glass has a grey tinge and is usually spotted with age.

At the turn of the 17th century, there was a vogue for hanging up decorative, silvered glass balls to reflect the room. Their original name of 'watch ball' has been corrupted into **witche's ball**.

THE MATERIALS

The main component of glass is silica, which is derived from sand or flint, sometimes crushed rock. As the melting temperature of silica (2,000 degrees Centigrade) is far higher than anything that could be attained by primitive methods, a form of alkaline flux was needed to lower that melting point. For this, the ancients (at first unwittingly) used a basic sodium carbonate called natrun, found at Wadhi Natrun in the Western Desert, Egypt. The ancient Syrians also used potash for their flux, made from the ash produced by burning the appropriately named plant, glasswort. This alkali, known as 'Syrian ash', with the addition of a little limestone or chalk, was the basis of **soda glass**.

This formula remained in use until a chemical substitute was discovered in the late 18th century.

A glass to rival rock crystal (a transparent quartz) was every glass maker's goal, and one that was first achieved by Angelo Barovier in the mid-15th century in Murano. Instead of sand, Barovier used crushed pebbles to make **crystal** or **flint glass**. Another factor contributing to the superiority of this glass was the rediscovery of something the Egyptians had known in the 2nd millennium BC, that the addition of a little manganese neutralizes the adverse effect of the iron impurities in the silica. The process was jealously guarded, and no Venetian glass maker was allowed to work outside Murano.

In 16th-century England, home-produced glass had declined in favour of imported Venetian glass. In 1570 John le Carré, a gentleman verrier from Lorraine, came to England with three other families to manufacture Anglo-Venetian soda glass. He was succeeded by a Dutchman of Venetian birth, Giacomo Verzelini who, in 1575, was granted a licence to produce 'Venice glass'. Verzelini and his continental workers are considered the founders of English glass.

The next landmark in English glass manufacture was the development of **lead crystal** (known contemporarily as 'flint glass'). George Ravenscroft (1618–81), was a London merchant who imported glass from Antwerp and Venice. He also owned a factory in the Savoy, London, and had the use of an experimental factory in Henley-on-Thames. There he experimented with a new type of glass using lead as the flux. The initial results were poor, as the glass developed a crazed effect called 'crizzling'. The final version, the right mixture of silica, potash, saltpetre and red lead, worked well. Examples of Ravenscroft glass occasionally carry his mark, a raven's head, as a guarantee of quality. One unique property of Ravenscroft glass is that it turns completely white when wet.

English glass making was entirely changed by Ravenscroft's invention. Being that much heavier and softer than soda glass, lead crystal was easily cut and engraved. More important, it was a brilliant reflector of light and, at a stroke, replaced the rock crystal that had formerly been used in chandeliers.

The ancient Egyptians were fine exponents of the art of making **coloured** glass, and perfect examples of bottles survive in many colours – yellow, blue, green, purple and white. Coloured glass continued to be made through the centuries. In England glass makers were more concerned with clarity than colour, although coloured glass was made for stained-glass windows. Drinking glasses with coloured bowls are rare before 1750, but by 1800 they were quite common. Green was the most popular colour, although blue, amethyst and, later, shades of brown were all used.

Different additives have been used at different times to opacify glass. The Romans used antimony, while glass-makers in the 16th century added fluorspar (the same fluoride that is found in toothpaste) in the form of calcium fluoride. With lead crystal, tin oxide or arsenic were the preferred additives by the mid-18th century, producing a fine **opaque** glass to imitate porcelain, which was often used for clock faces.

The term **Bristol Blue** is generally over-worked to describe all blue glass. Much in fact came from elsewhere, and pre-dated the first recorded blue glass from Bristol (1763). The blue colour was achieved by the addition of cobalt oxide, called smalt, which was imported from Saxony through the port of Bristol where it was sold at auction. As the city was the only source of cobalt, the better quality blue glass was known as Bristol Blue, wherever it was made, so perpetuating the myth that it was all made there. Some glass-makers, such as I. Jacobs and his son, signed their work with their names and the word 'Bristol'.

In the late 18th century a glassworks making bottles was founded by John Lucas in the village of Nailsea, a few miles south-west of Bristol. He is more famous, however, for his sideline of making all manner of domestic articles, such as jugs and rolling pins, decorated with strands of coloured glass, often flecked, sometimes splashed, in white. Later came 'bygones' and friggers (qv), such as witches' balls, glass tobacco pipes and walking sticks. As a consequence, all glass of this type is given the sobriquet Nailsea, regardless of origin.

Mosaic or **millefiori** glass was made as early as the

2nd millennium BC, and was widely produced by Roman glass makers. Here, short, thin 'canes' of coloured glass were set around an inner clay core, and held in place with an outer layer of clay. The glass and clay was then fired, annealed (cooled) and the clay casing and mould chipped away, leaving a solid glass piece. The art was rediscovered by Venetian glass-makers in the 16th century who gave it the name, *millefiori*, meaning many flowers, which describes its patterns. Millefiori was very popular in the 19th century, particularly in the making of paper weights in Bohemia, France, England and America.

THE DECORATION

The art of creating **cut glass** dates from pre-Roman times, when vessels were cut with stone wheels. The process probably first came to England from Bohemia in the early 17th century. Being heavy and thick, English lead crystal was admirably suited for such decoration and was widely used from the 1720s. The glass was not literally cut, but the surface was ground away by a rotating iron wheel, at first operated by treadle, then by water power, and in the 19th century by steam power.

The decoration to be cut was drawn into the glass, the lines followed by the cutter looking through the glass. The designs were generally geometric – dia-monds, triangles, or facets of six or eight sides. The

A glass beaker with a threaded decoration, c.1600

115

work was done freehand and curves, though not impossible, were difficult to achieve. Once the initial cuts had been roughed out they were finished with a smaller wheel, then polished by wooden or cork wheels and pumice.

The Excise Act of 1745 exacted a heavy tax on glass manufacture, thereby altering the glass making practices in England. The tax was levied on the weight of glass to be cast, rather than on the finished article. As a result the lead content of lead crystal was reduced and much thinner glass was produced. Thinner glass meant shallower cut glass. Only the rich could now afford heavy glass. Another effect of the Act was to encourage manufacturers into other decorative areas, such as coloured glass, engraving, gilding and painting.

The most far-reaching effect of the later 1777 Excise Act was to stimulate the Irish glass industry. Ireland was exempt from these punitive taxes, but also forbidden to export her wares. After the American War of Independence, free trade abolished these restrictions in Ireland and the famous factories of Waterford, Dublin, and Cork flourished by exporting large quantities of glass to England. Without the duty, their lead crystal could be cheaper and heavier, with deeper cutting. The English glass industry suffered, with workers emigrating to Ireland and France, until the tax was finally repealed in 1835. By the end of the 19th century glass cutting had been revived, with a profusion of deep cuts in straight lines to produce diamonds and stars.

Glass has been decorated by **engraving** since the 1st millennium BC, the design made by a revolving stone wheel. A more sophisticated form of wheel engraving, using copper discs operated by a treadle, was developed in the early 17th century in Prague. Soon after, Nuremberg became the centre of glass engraving, renowned throughout Europe for its excellent work. Still finer forms were **relief** engraving, where the background was cut away like a cameo, and **intaglio** engraving, the exact reverse, where the design is cut into the background.

Since they were first introduced in 16th-century

Venice, diamonds have traditionally been used for engraving on glass. The process was refined in the 18th century by a Dutchman, Frans Greenwood, who perfected stipple engraving, where a diamond-ended stick was tapped against the glass, leaving a series of minute dots to form the decoration. The closer the dots, the darker the background. This method was used by all skilled glass engravers, such as Lawrence Whistler, to great effect. Steel engraving, where the glass is tapped with a steel tip, is considered inferior.

Sand-etching or **sand-blasting** as a means of decorating glass was developed in the United States towards the end of the 19th century. A template was either cut out of a piece of strong paper and fixed to the glass for simple designs, or the glass was covered with a stiff paint and the design scratched away for more intricate patterns. A fine jet of sand was then directed on to the exposed glass at a high velocity. The result was somewhat crude. Although it was known in the 16th century that certain acids would attack glass, **acid-etching** was not developed until the early 1800s. For this, the glass was covered in beeswax and the design scratched away. It was then immersed in hydrofluoric acid which ate into the exposed areas of the glass. When the required depth of decoration was achieved, the glass was removed and cleaned. Often, etched glass was further embellished by fire gilding.

Gilding has been a common form of glass decoration since Roman times. In its simplest form, gold leaf was applied to the glass with one of a vast variety of 'mordants', such as gum arabic, gelatine, even egg white. In the 17th century glass was gilded with gold leaf, then covered with a film of powdered glass and fired.

THE STYLES

As both the Venetian *crystallo*, or soda glass, and potash glass set quickly, they could be blown very thin into drinking vessels, or manipulated into elaborate shapes. Lead crystal, on the other hand, with its lower melting point, was more viscous and therefore malleable for a longer period. Consequently, English glass designs tend to be more rounded. Typical is the **baluster-stem** glass of the early 18th century. This stem was made from a molten blob, or gather, that formed naturally into a baluster shape as it fell off the end of the pontil. With this basic shape, the embellishments were endless. The type of decoration is the first clue to dating.

Early baluster-stem glasses of the 18th century were plain, the baluster usually inverted with the wider part at the top. Later came the addition of knops, or 'swellings' on the stem – either under the bowl, called a cushion, in the middle, or above the foot, called a base knop. These knops took many forms, mostly self-descriptive, such as round balls, eggs, acorns, or mushrooms. Knop glasses were often further decorated by cutting or engraving.

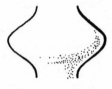

Angular knop   *Drop knop*

Tear-stem glasses were made by indenting the molten glass and covering it with another layer of glass. The trapped air-bubble was then drawn out and shaped into a tear, a comma, or inverted into a pear shape. This style was prevalent from c.1715 to c.1760.

A clever variation of the baluster-stem glass, made between 1715 and 1765, was a glass with a **moulded pedestal** or **Silesian stem**. This was made by pouring molten glass into a short six- or eight-sided mould, often with a decoration such as a star or simple flower on the bottom. The cooled stump was then reheated, and drawn out into a multi-sided baluster stem, the impressed motif appearing either under the bowl or above the foot. After 1725, baluster-stem glasses became more delicate, with lighter stems and smaller knops, which by mid-century were often no more than a bump.

One form of decoration to the stem of a lead crystal glass was the **air-twist**, first made from about the mid-18th century. Once the bowl had been blown, a short cylindrical stub of gather was picked up on the pontil and the end pierced with two or more round nails. The bowl was then attached to this indented stub, so trapping the beads of air inside the holes. The stem was then heated again, drawn out and twisted at the same time, the trapped air forming a spiral of silvery 'threads'. The term **Mercury-twist** is more descriptive than accurate, and was used for glasses that were in fashion from c.1745 to c.1765. They were formed in exactly the same way as an air-twist, only using fatter nails or, more often, making a pair of slits with a knife so that the refraction of the corkscrew twist in the lead crystal gave the effect of a ribbon of mercury. On an **incised-twist** glass, (c.1678–1780) the stem was twisted like a tightly coiled rope.

Another variation of the twist glass in the mid-18th century was the **opaque-twist** stem, also known as thread-twist, or enamel-twist. Short rods of white glass (also known as enamels) were set in a circular mould, covered with clear, molten glass, then allowed to cool. The result was re-heated and twisted as it was drawn out, so forming a delicate spiral inside. Lengths of up to 70 feet could be achieved from one mould. This long rod was then cut into lengths for individual stems. Coloured stems were made by using a coloured rod, either red, blue, green or yellow, with white to make **colour-twist** glasses: with a combination of many colours, it was called a **tartan-twist**. Another variation was the combination of opaque and air-twists. Opaque twists were also made on the Continent, where the spiral turned both ways – in England, the spiral went only clockwise up the stem.

Until the early 1770s quality glass was solely for the rich, but from then on the **facet-stem** glass was made. This glass was simple and inexpensive to make, and the cut decoration to the stem, a series of hexagons, diamonds, scales or flutings, was applied later, in an inexpensive, semi-skilled operation. The style lasted until the 1790s.

THE TYPES

DRINKING GLASSES

As today, the household inventories of the 18th and 19th centuries listed special glasses for wines, spirits, ales and sweetmeats, the size and style of each of these being influenced by the reigning fashion.

Ale, the most popular drink for all classes until the end of the 18th century, was from the 17th century onwards drunk in the dining room from **ale** glasses. The shape of the true ale glass was a tall flute, often with a wrythen (spiral) moulding around the lower half of the bowl, usually with a short stem. Ale glasses after 1740 were often engraved with hop or barley motifs.

Ale glasses

Unlike modern wine glasses that differentiate between wines, the shape and style of **wine** glasses until the mid-18th century followed the prevailing fashion, but was determined by neither the colour nor the origin of the wine. The glass that resembles the modern champagne glass, with its hemispherical, flat bowl was not for wine but was the top bowl of a glass pyramid (qv).

The römer or **roemer** (a near spherical green bowl on a flared, conical, hollow base made from a single, coiled glass rod) was a common wine glass in the Rhineland and the Netherlands. Dating originally from the 16th century, it appeared in England in the 18th century. The roemer is not, however, the ancestor of the 18th-century **rummer**, in either name or shape, as the term comes from the German *Roemishe*, meaning Roman. Rummers were the most versatile of glasses, used for all

A rummer   *Cordial glasses*

manner of drinks. The bowl was large, and the rim for
the first time was larger than the base. The short stem
was another characteristic.

Spirits were drunk neat in small **dram** glasses
throughout the 18th century. These were small glasses
of various shapes, known variously as a nip, a joey, or
a ginette.

Liqueurs and cordials were both fashionable drinks
of the 18th and 19th centuries and were drunk from
cordial glasses. These were at least six inches high,
with comparatively small bowls. Similar was the **ratafia**
glass, named after the sweet liqueur, often drunk at
tea-time, that resembled curaçao flavoured with
almond or peach and cherry kernels. Although a nice
notion, there is no credence to the story that it was
called ratafia after the practice of lawyers drinking it in
celebration after a contract had been ratified! The bowl
was very small in accordance with the fashion, and
because the liqueur was extremely strong.

Water was drunk from water glasses, while the
wash-hand glass was the forerunner of the finger bowl.

Until the 19th century drinking glasses were not
set on the dining table, but kept on the sideboard (qv)
for a servant to fill and hand to the diner as required. It
was an unsatisfactory arrangement, and often the only
way to be given a drink was to offer a toast. The
toastmaster's or hostess glass was for those who
needed to reply to a toast, but did not want to
over-indulge. It was a small, apparently ordinary glass,
but with a thicker inside so holding less liquid. A
sham dram was similar, with a thick bowl that
magnified the contents. It was used by unscrupulous

landlords. When it was the custom at dinner to knock the table with the glass instead of clapping, a short, heavy based **firing** glass was used, so named as the rapping sound on the table resembled musket fire.

The aptly named **coin** glass had a coin set into the stem, or under the bowl. As earlier coins were frequently used, the date on the coin is no guarantee as to the date of manufacture of the glass.

Some of the earliest commemorative glasses were those engraved in the 18th century for the Jacobite cause, in support of the descendants of James II. These **Jacobite** glasses were usually for wine or ratafia, although other glassware such as tankards and jugs were also decorated in this fashion. Glasses in the style of the period were engraved with Jacobite emblems commemorating the rebellions of 1715 and 1745. The most common decorations were the six-petalled rose, rose buds, oak leaves, carnations, daffodils, fritillaries and, of course, the Scottish thistle. The jay, bee, butterfly or triple ostrich plumes were further motifs. Very rare were the portraits of the two Pretenders themselves. These motifs were often supported with Latin tags, such as *fiat* (may it be so), *redeat* (may he return), or *turnus tempo erit* (events will be changed). **Amen** glasses are engraved with verses of the Jacobite anthem.

Where a glass has no foot it is known as a **stirrup** or **coaching** glass. Dating from the 1830s, these were most often funnel-shaped, and used for 'stirrup cups', a fortifying drink taken at hunt meets or in coaches, where they did not need to be set down.

DECANTERS

Until the 17th century, wine was stored in barrels and transferred to the table in pewter, copper or ceramic flagons. The earliest glass bottles, which were used solely for serving wine, appeared towards the middle of the century. These early **bottle** decanters were of heavy, black glass, hemispherical in shape with a long neck. Occasionally they had a seal, bearing a date or some clue as to the owner, such as an Oxbridge college. Soon wine was decanted and stored in bottles, with a ring of glass welded around the neck to secure the string holding the stopper in place. These stoppers were either conical-shaped corks or pieces of oiled hemp.

A bottle decanter of blackish-green glass, with a seal, c.1720

By the end of the 17th century there were two distinct styles for decanters. One was modelled on a jug, with a handle, long neck and a spout; the other, which was more common, resembled a bottle, with a neck ring and a 'kick', a conical indentation in the base. This kick was initially part of the annealing (cooling) process in the making of the decanter, but it was later found to be useful for trapping the sediment of the wine. Decanters, unlike bottles, were made of clear glass, often with a loose glass stopper. The style was revived in the early 19th century.

The shape of the decanter changed with fashion. The **mallet** decanter (c.1705–30), was named after a sculptor's mallet which it resembled, and the **Prussian** decanter (c.1775–1830) was shaped like a barrel with three rings on the neck. Although the neck rings were superfluous once glass stoppers had been introduced, they were retained for decoration and ease of handling.

One constant shape was that of the **ship's** decanter. This heavy decanter from the mid-18th century had a very broad base, sloping in to a narrow neck to give it greater stability in a rolling sea. A variant of this was the **Rodney** decanter, which was more elaborate, often with stepped sides. It was named after Admiral Rodney in honour of his victory over the French fleet at the battle of Cape St Vincent in 1780.

From 1745 decanter **stoppers** were ground. Their shape also changed with fashion: late 18th-century stoppers are spire-shaped, by the turn of the century they are bull's-eye or target-shaped, while the mushroom-shaped stopper dates from c.1790–1840.

A decanter and stopper, cut with panels of 'strawberry diamond', early 19th century

During the Regency period there was a vogue for **coloured** decanters, usually made in sets of three and often with a gilded cartouche, or label, denoting the spirit inside – brandy, rum or Hollands (gin). There was no whisky, which was not a fashionable drink in England until the 1880s. Wines were similarly labelled. These decanters were made in two imperial sizes, either a pint or a quart.

By the end of the 18th century, glass manufacture had improved so much that glass could be made to withstand hot liquid without cracking. At the same time, rum became a popular drink, especially in a hot toddy – a mixture of rum, lemon juice, nutmeg and spices – which was drunk from a small, thick glass with a handle called a **toddy** glass. It was served by means of a **toddy lifter**, an ingenious device shaped like a small decanter with a long neck, whose bottom was open. The toddy lifter was lowered into the hot toddy, which flooded into its open bowl. The thumb was then put over the top, the air-pressure preventing the liquid from running out. When the thumb was removed, the drink flowed into the glass.

White wine was traditionally drunk chilled, having been cooled in ice in a cellaret (qv). The glasses, too, were cooled, either collectively in a Monteith (qv) or in individual **wine glass coolers**, cylindrical tubs with two distinct lips on the rim from which to hang the glasses, containing iced water to cool the glasses and to rinse them in between courses when dining informally.

TABLEWARE

Cut or engraved glass gave a certain refinement to the 18th- and 19th-century dining table, particularly when lit by candle-light. Glass **centrepiece** decorations were similar in style and purpose to those of silver, and in many cases, like the standing cup, actually replaced them on the table. Glass **epergnes** (qv) were also similar to those in silver and designed with equal fantasy but, being glass, were more easily broken and therefore fewer have survived.

An epergne

The dessert course was where glass really came into its own on the table. From the 18th century onwards, the tablecloth was removed after the first two dinner courses, and the mahogany table laid specially for the dessert. Apart from the epergne, with its arms carrying little dishes of crystallized fruit or whatever, the most important piece of glass was the **pyramid**, a series of glass salvers or trays, standing on stems (decorated in the style of the day), one on top of the other. There were usually three of four tiers, (larger ones could have as many as six), all surmounted with a 'top glass' or 'orange glass' (as it usually held an orange, fresh or preserved) on the very top. On each tier was a different dessert. There were dry or wet sweetmeats, and also fruit jellies, made from either calves' foot, 'isinglass' made from sturgeon, or 'hartshorn' from deer antlers, which were served in tall, bell-shaped glass bowls, often on four short feet. There were comfits, nuts and fruit, either fresh or crystallized, and custard, made from egg yolk, cream and some flavouring, served in a cup-shaped **custard** glass with one, occasionally two, handles. Syllabubs, made from cream flavoured with a fruit and white wine, were served in a wide-rimmed **syllabub** glass.

Spices have always played a major part in dining, and these additives and sauces appeared on the table in bottles and containers. Small individual glass cellars of the 18th century had heavy cut-glass bowls and square 'lemon- squeezer' bases. Sauces such as catsup and anchovy, and the spices pepper and kyan (cayenne), all had their own style of bottle that was usually part of a cruet (qv).

FRIGGERS

A **frigger** is a glassmaker's term for any item made up in his spare time from leftover materials, usually in coloured glass. They would be extremely intricate – a sailing ship with full rigging, a complete fox hunt, or birds perched in a tree – or comparatively simple – a bell, a walking stick, crowns, or a rolling pin.

During the Napoleonic Wars, salt was an expensive commodity which was taxed at a rate of 30 times its cost. It was sold in a **salt tube**, a bottle of thick, heavy glass with round nobs at each end. The earliest date from c.1800. Being heavy and with two natural handles, they doubled as rolling pins. Later salt tubes were made in coloured glass, often with some engraved or gilded motif as ornament.

In the late 17th century small, spherical bottles were blown with long necks, filled with holy water and hung in the house to ward off evil influences. They became symbols of good luck, and in the 18th century were blown as coloured **balls**, often enlivened with apt, scriptural texts. The Nailsea factory (qv) glass balls had a variety of decorations – air-thread spirals, spots, marbling, even transfer printing. Like the mirrored watch balls (qv), these were the forerunners of the glass balls that decorate the Christmas tree today.

CHANDELIERS

The term **chandelier**, like the object, is of medieval origin, and was used to describe lights with branches hanging from the ceiling or roof. The magnificent 18th-century glass chandelier is the successor of the **candle beam** and the **corona**, a circular iron hoop with either spikes or 'prickets' for candles, or individual cups for oil. Until the early 18th century, chandeliers were usually made of brass or silver (qv), the alternatives, rock crystal or the floral Venetian fantasies, being very expensive. Throughout the 18th and early 19th century, England and Ireland led the world in luminaria (light fittings), with their superior cut lead crystal drops that well imitated the rock crystal they replaced. There can be no finer chandeliers than those designed by Adam (qv) for the Penrose glass house in Waterford, Ireland, with, according to Klein, 'their sweeping, notched arms, the spires, canopies, and finials, the swags of glittering drops, the great spherical all-over-cut bodies, and the pans and nozzles [the actual candle holder] cut into points'. Because of the expense of candles, chandeliers were only used on very special occasions, the owner preferring to make do most of the time with smaller candlesticks.

Chandeliers would often have a matching candelabrum with two or more arms, and table lights for a single candle. The deep cutting and the refractive quality of the lead crystal glass made for a wonderful effect. A **girandole** candlestick of the 18th century has a circle of lustres (crystal drops) hanging from the flange.

MIRRORS

During the 17th century the size of the looking glass was governed by the limitations of manufacture of the glass itself. As most mirrored glass was still being made in small panes, these small looking glasses were set into disproportionately large frames, often of carved wood, tortoiseshell or stump work (qv), to make the most of this expensive luxury. Mirrors were also made to stand on dressing tables as part of the toilet set. The Puritans banned the manufacture of mirrors during the Commonwealth as an 'aid to vanity'. Towards end of the 17th century looking glasses became slightly larger, mostly with square 'cushion' frames of walnut veneer (qv), marquetry (qv), lacquer (qv), even silver.

With the advent of casting sheet glass at the end of the 17th century, the looking glass became a decorative piece in its own right, rather than just a means to show off an elaborate frame. Glass from the 'smallest size upwards, to 90 Inches, with proportionable width with Lively Colours, free from Veins and foulness', was being manufactured at a number of glassworks around London. The Duchess of Portsmouth, mistress of Charles II, even had a mirrored room. The **pier glass** was a large sheet of mirrored glass designed to fit in the 'pier', the wall between two windows, and was introduced in the late 17th century. It hung above a pier table (qv) to reflect the candle-light at night and the daylight by day.

Throughout the 18th and 19th centuries looking glass frames followed the prevailing style and were either gilded or, as in the case of Queen Anne, walnut-veneered. In the mid-18th century the chimney-glass or **chimney-piece** mirror was introduced from France. These were often square and made in three parts, the centre being twice the width of the outside two. Occasionally an oil painting was substituted for the centre panel. A narrow mirror set at the bottom of a painting in the dining room is thought to be for the butler to keep an eye on the table without obviously intruding on the dinner.

Sheraton (qv) is credited with the introduction of a **tabernacle** mirror, which has a row of balls surmounted on a flat cornice above a painted scene on glass or canvas, with columns on either side. These mirrors were popular in the United States where their owners claimed that they were not mirrors but pictures, to escape the punitive tax on glass.

A fashionable mirror at the end of the 18th century was subsequently called the **Regency** mirror. With either a concave or, more usually, convex glass, these mirrors were invariably circular. They could be either plain or ornate with a gilt, carved frame, usually decorated with balls, and surmounted with foliated scrolls. On the top was a carved motif, most commonly an eagle, sometimes a phoenix or Ho-Ho bird. Other birds and animals drifted in and out of fashion, like the crocodile after 1798 in celebration of Nelson's victory over the French at the Battle of the Nile. They were also known as bull's-eye mirrors.

A circular mirror with a carved frame surmounted by an eagle, c.1800

While looking glasses in the main reception rooms were purely for decoration and to spread light, in the bedroom they were an essential part of the furniture. The small **toilet glass** of the early 18th century stood on the dressing table or chest, either mounted on two uprights on long feet or on a box base with one or three drawers. With another earlier style, the mirror was mounted in the lid of a dressing box which also had small compartments for jewellery or toilet accessories

Towards the end of the 18th century the large free-standing toilet mirror on two uprights supported on long feet was known as a **cheval** mirror, or occasionally as a 'Psyche' after the beautiful maiden loved by Cupid, often portrayed with a looking glass. These full-length looking glasses were supported on a tilting mechanism called a 'horse', although some moved up and down, according to Sheraton, 'the same as a sash window'.

Gentlemen shaved at a hinged, circular, concave **shaving glass** mounted on a tripod stand. Some in the late 18th century had a magnifying lens that could be moved in front of the glass.

METALWORK

INTRODUCTION

The art of working in metal originated in prehistoric times, as the Bronze and Iron Ages, named after the discovery and working of those base metals, testify. That said, gold was worked in the Stone Age but, being so soft, it had no use other than for decoration and ornament. Nor have the basic techniques of metal-working altered for centuries. Put a Roman metal-worker in a blacksmith's workshop today, and he could begin work almost immediately. As a craft, metalwork overlaps with many others: furniture without the metal-worker's skill would be basic and unadorned, architecture unthinkable. There would be no jewellery. Other trades, too, rely on the metal-worker's skill, to produce for example the joiner's and furniture maker's tools, the tailor's scissors and the butcher's knives.

THE CRAFT

The working of metal can be divided into four main techniques: casting, forging, sheet-metalwork and benchwork. Casting is when molten metal is poured into moulds of varying complexity, from a simple form in the ground to the intricate moulds required for casting sculpture.

Forging, the heating and shaping of metal, is mainly confined to wrought iron. The iron is heated and beaten into shape – either lengthened (drawing out) or short-ened (jumping up) – while perforations are made by hammering. The iron can also be twisted and bent into shapes by hammering it over an anvil or a form, and two red-hot pieces are welded together by hammering.

Sheet-metalwork is the fashioning of metal once it has been rolled out into thin sheets. It is either cut, hammered or rolled into shape. The pieces are joined by either braising, riveting or soldering. Sheet-metalwork

131

is easily decorated, whether engraved, chased, pierced or embossed (where the design is punched out from the back). When an embossed piece is further worked from the front, it is called **repoussé**, a method widely used in the 18th century.

With **benchwork**, the metal is worked cold, either filed or chiselled into shape and drilled. The practice is also called 'locksmithery' as locks and keys are made in this way.

THE MATERIALS

The uses of **iron** vary according to its carbon content. If it has more than 4% carbon, it is fit only for casting, hence its name **cast iron**. With less carbon it becomes **steel**, much favoured by the early locksmiths. It can be hardened by heating and sudden cooling. Iron in its purest form can be easily worked with heat, when it is known as **wrought iron**. Iron has been continuously worked in England, with few changes, since before the Roman occupation. Most of the surviving medieval wrought ironwork is classed as builder's hardware – hinges and hasps – as opposed to that which is both functional and decorative, such as railings, gates and balconies. Cast pieces were generally confined to the fireplace or stove.

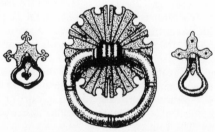

Tudor wrought iron door knockers

The term base metals includes the natural elements of copper, lead, zinc and tin (as opposed to the precious metals of gold, silver, platinum and titanium). Base metals are combined to make alloys. **Bronze** is an alloy of copper and tin. **Brass** is an alloy of copper and calamine (a zinc carbonate), while **latten** is similar but with a small percentage of tin. Like brass, it was cast (Henry VIII's tomb is of latten) or used in sheet form. Different ratios produce different alloys: **pinchbeck**, named after a watchmaker, Christopher Pinchbeck (1670–1732), is an alloy of five parts copper to two parts zinc, which resembles gold. It was used for cheap jewellery, watch cases and other *objets de vertu*.

In England **ormolu** and **mosaic gold** were other brass alloys that resembled gold in colour and so did not require extra gilding. Ormolu (from the French *d'orure d'or moulu*, meaning literally 'gilding with gold paste') was used in the late 18th century in the manufacture of vases, candlesticks, even door furniture. These were gilded with an amalgam, an alloy of mercury and gold that was painted on to the piece, then fired to drive off the mercury (giving off a lethal smoke). This process was also known as fire-gilding.

Pewter, depending on its age and quality, is an amalgam of either tin and copper (the best and most commonly used today), or of tin and antimony (a silvery, brittle chemical element with a low melting point) or, the least good, of tin and lead. **Britannia metal**, a hard form of pewter which is an alloy of antimony and copper was widely used in the 19th century. After 1840, it was used for electroplating and stamped 'EPBM' – electro-plated Britannia metal.

The 'silver' coins of today are made from an alloy of 75% copper and 25% nickel. German silver, also known as **nickel-silver**, is brass mixed with 30% nickel and when electroplated is stamped 'EPNS' – electroplated nickel silver. Resembling silver is **paktong**, an alloy of copper, nickel and zinc that was widely used in Chinese furniture. In England it was used for candlesticks and fire grates from the end of the 18th century onwards.

Pure zinc, known as **spelter**, was used for casting small pieces more normally associated with bronze, but was far cheaper to produce. Many factories, particularly in Berlin, produced a variety of sculptures, such as animals and birds, and would often dust the pieces with bronze powder to make to make them look grander than they actually were.

Because of its ease of working and low melting point, **lead** has been worked since Roman times for decorative and functional work. The Elizabethans used cast lead rainwater ware – downpipes, hoppers and water troughs. Garden statuary, vases, urns and fountains were all made in lead from this period onwards. Pollution in the air has taken its toll of much fine lead sculpture.

Copper in its purest form is difficult to cast, and consequently it is invariably used in an alloy. Sheet copper, however, is easily worked and has been used for household wares for centuries. The copper sheet could be beaten into any shape and soldered or riveted together.

THE DECORATION

ENAMELLING

The term **enamelling** describes the process of applying a powdered glass mixture, coloured by metallic oxides mixed with fusing agents, to a metal base. This base was generally copper, although brass was an alternative for larger pieces, gold and silver for finer work, such as snuff boxes and jewellery. The technique of enamelling has been known since the 13th century BC, and was widely used for religious artifacts between the 9th and 12th century in the Byzantine Empire.

The most common form of enamelling is *cloisonné*, where thin strips or wire, either copper or gold (known as *cloisons*), were soldered on to the metal base following the lines of a pattern. These 'enclosures' were then over-filled with the different coloured enamels, and fired in a kiln. Different metallic oxides fuse at different temperatures, so the enamellers were either particularly skilled, or trusted to trial and error. The fired piece was ground flat, the *cloisons* being polished or gilded to produce a jewel-like effect. Where the 'enclosures' are formed within the metal base, by either punching or engraving, it is known as *champlevé*. Another skilful variation of *cloisonné* dating from the 14th century and widely used in jewellery is *plique à jour*. As with *cloisonné*, the enameller follows the pattern in wire, but with a clay base the enamel does not adhere. The finished effect is like a stained-glass window. In the 16th century, masters developed enamels that could be painted on to the base metal without having to be separated by metal strips. The result was **Limoges** painted enamel. Both the French and the English enamellers of the mid-18th century found that curving the surface to be enamelled overcame the problem of the enamel cracking as it expanded at a different rate to the base metal.

JAPANNING

The art of **japanning**, stimulated during the Restoration by the passion of the time for Oriental lacquerwork, was contemporarily defined as 'the covering of wood or metals by grounds of opaque colours in varnish which, when varnished and dried, may afterwards be decorated with painted ornament, in gold and colours, or left plain'.

At the end of the 17th century, the town of Bilston in Staffordshire was noted for fine quality japanning work on metal, mostly highly decorated snuff boxes. In the same period, the trade was also practised by a family called Allgood from Pontypool, Monmouthshire. Such was the quality of their japanning that **Pontypool**, or Pontipool, later became the generic name for this type of work. The Allgoods used the best sheet-iron, formed into the required article and coated in molten tin that penetrated the iron. The tinned iron piece was then painted with a characteristic ground colour (usually scarlet, green, yellow, black or white) in a 'japan', an asphaltum varnish, and fired in an oven. The process was repeated several times. The decoration was then applied, usually floral swags, flowers and landscapes. Several coats of clear varnish were finally applied, each coat being rubbed down and fired for long periods. The result was extremely hard, even fireproof, which made it good for all manner of domestic wares such as tea trays, candlesticks, tea and coffee urns, chestnut warmers, kettles and charcoal burners for smokers. In the early 18th century large factories were set up in Birmingham and Wolverhampton to mass-produce Pontypool japanned ware. The industry died out towards the end of the 19th century, when it was superseded by electro-plated (qv) goods.

Japanning on sheet-iron was also common in France in the mid-18th century, where it was called *tôle*, hence the subsequent English term **tôleware**, used to describe any tin article that had been japanned. *Tôle de cuivre* was applied to sheet-copper, and *tôle peinte* was painted ware. Some early *tôle* blanks were sent to Canton to be painted in the Oriental style. This highly decorative work was used for a diverse selection of objects, from trays to inkwells, urns to jardinières.

THE TYPES

FIREPLACE AND SMOKING EQUIPMENT

Being non-combustible and durable, the prime uses of iron, brass and copper were connected with the fire and the fireplace.

In the medieval great hall, the fireplace was a slab of stone or iron in the centre of the room, called a down-hearth. When the fire was moved against the wall to the fireplace in the 13th century, the stones of the wall were heated so retaining warmth. As it was constantly in the fire, the back wall would have to be replaced from time to time, and when brick generally replaced stone for walls in the early 16th century, the fragile bricks were even more easily damaged. To protect them and to reflect the heat back into the room, the **fireback** (or reredos) made of cast iron was introduced. The earliest recorded fireback is dated 1548. These early firebacks came from those places, (Sussex, Kent and the Forest of Dean) where there was both a plentiful supply of timber for smelting and of iron ore. They were simple to cast. The design was first carved in wood which was impressed into an open, sand mould. The molten iron was poured into the mould, and left to cool.

Early designs were usually simple, often personalized with just the initials of the owner and the date. From the 17th century onwards the decoration was more elaborate. Armorial bearings and religious subjects were fashionable, particularly after the Commonwealth. Royal arms, or royal subjects, were also common, such as the representation of the Boscobel oak which hid Charles II after the Battle of Worcester in 1651. Firebacks have continued to be made in the same style for centuries and reproductions abound.

With both the central and the side fireplace, some method was required for keeping the burning logs from falling out on to the floor. For this a fire grate, sleepers (simple metal bars to raise the logs) or pairs of iron rests or **firedogs** were used. The original wrought iron firedog, dating from Roman times, had two uprights that splayed out into two legs, connected by a bar on which the logs rested. Later, the rear upright was reduced to the height of the bar. With **firecats**, the uprights were legs as well, so that, like a cat when dropped, they always landed on their feet.

Large firedogs (over 18 inches) are termed **andirons**. They may be fitted with hooks or pegs at the front to take a spit, and a circular support at the top for a basting bowl. The fire being the focal point of the room, andirons were frequently decorative as well. Cast iron andirons with a variety of decorations vary from the relatively simple Gothic taste of the 16th century, to the cast figures of notables of the day, soldiers and dolphins of the 19th century. Often, the andirons were embellished with brass finials, as much for decoration as to reflect light out of the fire. Occasionally they were made of silver, or silver with an iron core. When purely decorative, they were usually accompanied by firedogs.

'Sea coal' was burnt as early as the 17th century in a **fire-basket**, which rested on the firedogs. It was a

Andirons

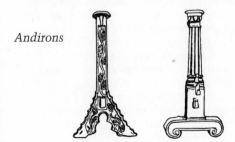

137

short step to unite the basket, firedogs and fireback to make the **dog-grate**. This was made predominately of iron, and styles were often very grand in the late 18th and 19th century. Robert Adam (qv) produced many designs for dog-grates in the neo-classical style.

From the earliest times to the early 19th century, it was the custom never to let the fire go out, even at night (some fires have been recorded to have burned continuously for over a century). At night, the fire was raked out and the embers covered with a **curfew**, (from the French *couvre feu*, meaning 'fire cover') to keep them glowing overnight. The curfew was a simple brass or copper hood, with a handle on top, and quatrespherical (a quarter of a sphere) in shape. It was often beautifully embellished with chased and repoussé (qv) decoration. The other meaning of the word curfew, a time after dark when people are forbidden to go outside, originates from this practice.

The glowing embers were revived through a fire blower or **blowing tube**, a simple, tapering brass or iron tube with a mouthpiece at one end and a perforated spike at the other. It was used rather like a pea-shooter, so that, when blown, the concentrated air had a similar effect to **bellows**. An ingenious device that came from Ireland in the 17th century was the pair of **peat bellows**, where the draught was created by a series of paddles rotated by turning a handle.

Something akin to the smaller firedogs was used to take the 'chimney furniture' or **fire-irons** – shovel, fork, poker and tongs. From the Restoration onwards, these were made in sets in brass or, according to John Evelyn in 1690, silver as 'Iron is now quite out of date'. The **fend-iron** or fender of the 18th century was refined from the medieval fire-guard, and often matched the fire-irons as a set.

Whether in cottage or palace, the fire has always been the main source of heat (and partially, light) in a room, and many items are common to both abodes. One such piece was the **trivet**, a stand for vessels to keep them warm in front of the fire. Usually on three legs, earlier trivets were of iron, later ones of brass. A **footman** was an attractive four-legged trivet, with a brass top and pierced frieze, often with cabriole legs in front.

Designs for fire-irons by Pugin in the Gothic revival style, 1827

A pastime popular with all classes was roasting chestnuts in the fire. The early 18th-century **chestnut roasters** were made of sheet iron with a perforated lid and long, iron handles. Later models in brass are decorative fakes. The copper or brass **warming pan** was a late 16th-century invention that was made until the mid-19th century, when it was superseded by the stoneware hot water bottle. The round pan with a lid and long handle, filled with glowing embers or smouldering charcoal, was moved between the sheets to take the chill off the bed. The handle was either turned wood or steel, when it was probably Dutch. The lids of early pans were decoratively fretted to allow the heat to escape, while the later 18th-century pans tend to be plainer.

Tobacco came to Europe in 1560 from the New World. It was brought to France by the French ambassador to the Portuguese court, Jean Nicot, after whom it was named Nicotina. Despite its early prohibitive cost, smoking became popular with all classes, particularly after the first settlements in Virginia sent back leaf tobacco in the early 17th century.

For this new craze, metal smokers' equipment was

made in enormous quantities. **Pipe** or **ember tongs** were long, delicate tongs used to take lighted embers from the fire to light a pipe. Some opened with a spring mechanism, others, called lazy tongs, had an expanding, criss-cross mechanism. Those with a whistle were made for inns, and used to summon the staff. Most tongs were fitted with a small, round pad, called a **stopper**, used to tamp down the glowing tobacco in the pipe.

Brass is a good medium for casting, particularly small objects like **tobacco stoppers**. Made between the 17th and mid-19th century, these stoppers had a round base and an ornamental top of every conceivable design, including animals and the busts of the famous. Most popular was a well-turned lady's leg.

Metal pipes, made of sheet-iron, steel, brass and silver, date from the 16th century but, being impractical, were never as popular as clay pipes. The fashion in the early 19th century for smoking pipes made of silver while out hunting was, like the smokers themselves, short-lived.

LIGHTING

Until the advent of gas in the early 19th century, artificial light for domestic use came traditionally from three sources: solid fat coated on a wick, oil burned in lamps, and the ancient source of burning the wood of the seasoned fir tree split into 'candles'. Poorer homes burned rushes, a surprisingly good and very cheap source of light. The rushes were cut in mid-summer, their outer covers were stripped off, and they were dipped into mutton or bacon fat. The coated rush was held in the spring jaws of a **rushlight holder**, a simple device made of wrought iron by the local blacksmith, which stood on the floor or the table. The burning rush, about 28 inches long, gave a good clear light and lasted nearly an hour, although it was smelly and inclined to smoke.

Early candles were made of either tallow or wax, or a combination of both, formed around a cotton or flax wick. Spermaceti candles, made from the blubber of the sperm whale, appeared in the mid-18th century and gave a clear, even light. The medieval hall was lit by candles and flaming torches held in openwork cages or cressets. The candles could be mounted on a **candle beam**, an iron or wooden hoop suspended from the ceiling on a pulley, on wall brackets, or on a **candle-stand**, a secular version of an altar candlestick, made of brass or bronze, which stood on the floor and often had branches to hold several candles. Larger candles were supported on a 'pricket' or spike, and were made with a hole in the bottom for this purpose; smaller candles were held in a 'nozzle' or socket. Candle stands were reduced in size to become 'table-stands' for the table. The baluster shape of these **candlesticks** was inspired by those imported from Persia and the Middle East.

Candlesticks can be dated quite accurately by their design and method of construction, although there are, of course, many exceptions. Those made in the late 16th and 17th century were usually cast in brass, and called **trumpet-based** candlesticks, as their base was shaped like the end of a trumpet with a very wide drip pan on the stem. Most candlesticks made before 1700 were cast and finished off on a lathe; after that date, they were seamed, that is, cast in two halves and joined together. This made it easier to make the decorative knop, the 'swelling' on the stem. Octagonal bases can be dated between 1680 and 1720; those that are oblong with cut off corners are earlier, while those with square bases and cut off corners are later. **Flower** or **petal** bases came in about 1730. **Square** bases date from about 1760 and were popular for only a short time. **Round** bases came in about 1770, appearing again in the 1820s, although **oval** bases were fashionable in the 1780s.

The stem also gives a clue to the date. Before the 1740s stems tended to be well rounded; after that date they were more elaborate, often fluted and tapering. With a hollow stem, it was possible to have a 'pusher' or slide inside to dislodge the spent candle. If the stem was rolled brass, a lever could be inserted in the seam for the same purpose.

A candlestick on a small pan with a ring handle, was known as a **chamber-stick**. Like the silver version (qv), this 18th-century holder often had a built-in flint and tinder box, and a peg on which to hang the candle extinguisher or snuffer scissors. Later 19th-century examples had a glass flue.

Despite the enormous number of candlesticks made, fakes abound which can easily be spotted by looking inside the base. If the rough casting inside the stem has been smoothed off by turning, it is more likely to be genuine than if the base is still pitted straight from the cast.

The crude wall-mounted pricket bracket of the medieval hall developed into the ornate **sconce** of the 17th century. These were either silver (qv) or brass, highly polished to reflect the light from the candles. Where the backing of the sconce incorporates a glass mirror it is called a **girandole** (not to be confused with the American name for an eagle-mounted convex mirror).

The candle beams of the medieval hall developed into the multi-branched **chandelier**. As most brass or laten chandeliers were imported from the Low Countries, the Dutch influence on the English-made chandelier was strong. The design changed little during the 16th and 17th century, with its bulbous centre supporting the many arms with candle sockets. It was raised or lowered on pulleys. Later 18th-century brass chandeliers were very ornate, with anything up to twenty scrolling arms, and widely used, particularly in the grander churches.

Lamps for burning vegetable or mineral oil, usually through a floating wick, were common in ancient Egypt. Greek and Roman lamps, using the same principle, were often elaborate affairs in bronze or brass. The similar English lamp changed little until the early 17th century. This burned vegetable and fish oils (from the livers of fish, such as herring, cod, ling and hake) or animal fats, with wicks made from either hemp, cotton, moss or pith. The smell was dreadful.

Improvements to lamps suffered a setback with the imposition of the candle tax in 1709 (not repealed until 1831), which made it illegal to make candles at home or use oil lamps unless they burned fish oil. Nevertheless in 1784 a Swiss doctor, Aimé Argand, patented in England a hollow wick that overcame the problem of the current dim, foul-smelling, smoking oil

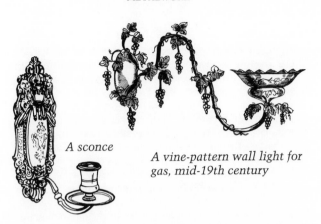

A sconce

A vine-pattern wall light for gas, mid-19th century

lamp. A further refinement added a glass tube over the flame. The **Argand oil lamp**, with an urn-shaped oil reservoir and glass chimney, was generally wall-mounted. The oil for these lamps tended to be expensive, either refined olive oil or spermaceti (whale oil). In 1836 the improved 'moderator' lamp appeared, where 'the oil was forced up by a large piston pressed by a spring on the whole body of the oil, which is prevented from flowing too quickly by a wire in the supply tube'. These lamps burned colza, an oil extracted from rape seed, which was cheap but not very illuminating. Camphine oil burned far brighter but, such was the volatility of the spirit, it exploded easily. The result was more exciting than convenient. The biggest breakthrough came with the discovery of mineral oils in the United States, and with this the manufacture of paraffin which superseded all other oils.

Although Pall Mall in London was lit in 1807 by carburetted hydrogen street lamps, or **gas lighting** as it was better known, gas was not used in domestic houses in towns until the 1840s, following the foundation of the Gas Light and Coke Company. Electricity too was first available in the 1840s. It could not, however, be harnessed for light until the invention of the filament bulb in the 1870s. It was another 50 years before it was available universally.

PEWTERWARE

Although the Romans brought pewter-work to Britain, there are few examples of English pewter dating from before the 13th century. The Pewterers' Company, which held the monopoly of the Cornish tin mines, was formed in the mid-14th century. From then on pewter began to replace natural components such as wood, leather and horn, for everyday articles like plates and dishes, flagons, beakers and tankards, spoons and candlesticks. Initially, pewter articles were for the rich only, but by the mid-17th century, they were widely available to all and exported in large quantities.

The Pewterer's Guild was a powerful regulatory body. Every master pewterer was required to register his personal mark with the Guild. As this was done by punching it on a 'touch plate', the stamp was called a touch mark. Often there is a date beside the mark but, unlike silver marks, this denotes the year of registration of the pewterer rather than the date of manufacture of the article. The popularity of pewter waned towards the end of the 18th century, as the Pewterers' Company lost control of quality standards by allowing the use of inferior materials, and demand grew for the more practical ceramic pieces.

Flatware. With their high lead content, the earliest pewter plates were only marginally safer than the unhygienic wooden trenchers they replaced. Pewter plates up to 12 inches in diameter were called 'sadware'; a 'dish' was between 12 and 18 inches in diameter, while a 'charger' was over 18 inches. Most sadware, such as the deep dish with a broad rim called a 'cardinal's hat', was plain. However, being soft and malleable it was easily cast, chased, hammered or punched in a variety of decorations. Spoons were the only cutlery that could be made of pewter, and they were manufactured in enormous numbers. The designs altered little over 300 years: the bowl was shallow and pear-shaped, the thin stem ending in some decorative motif, such as a simple ball, a figure of an Apostle, or a lion.

Hollow ware. The term 'hollow ware' describes all other shaped pieces, such as bowls, drinking vessels, flagons and measures. Pewter bowls for eating were particularly common, as were the early drinking vessels, beakers and tankards. These followed traditional shapes, the tankards having a handle and a lid with a thumb piece. A flagon was a taller, slender version of a tankard.

Early measures had been made of leather, and their bulbous bottle shape was copied when they were made in pewter. Their sizes varied, each county having its own measure until they were standardized into the Imperial Measure in 1826. Measures in similar shapes and sizes were also commonly made in copper. After 1826 they were usually made with a lead seal, often stamped with the initial of the reigning monarch.

Domestic ware. Pewter was used for many other household items such as whole tea services, candlesticks, inkwells, sand dredgers or pounce boxes, shakers filled with sand to dust down paper after writing on it.

LOCKS

In about 1,000 BC wooden locks were bartered by the Phoenicians in England for Cornish tin. These rudimentary **pin locks**, invented by the ancient Egyptians, had a simple bar operated with a key. The design was copied and remained the standard lock in the West Country until the mid-19th century. Thereafter metal locks, with a similar straight bolt operated by a tumbril action, were common, and by the 12th century London had become the centre of their manufacture. The mechanism barely altered until 1843, when an American, Linus Yale of Massachusetts, invented the **cylinder lock**.

Iron keyhole escutcheons, 17th century

The **rim lock** was mounted on the outside of the door and enclosed in an iron or brass casing that was often highly ornamented. The very heavy mahogany doors of the early 18th century were thick enough to take a **mortise lock,** which fitted within the timber. The **detector lock,** invented by the famous 18th-century locksmith John Wilkes of Birmingham, was an ingenious device that recorded on a dial the number of times that the door was opened.

Locks were always expensive, and consequently were treated as tenants' fixtures that could be removed at the end of the tenancy, as was all door furniture. The feud between Queen Anne and Sarah, Duchess of Marlborough, intensified after the Queen discovered that the duchess had removed the locks from her grace-and-favour apartments in St James's Palace, London. These were not, however, used on the front door of the Marboroughs' Blenheim Palace, as the magnificent lock there was copied (with the King of Poland's permission) for the 4th Duke of Marlborough from a gate in Warsaw.

SILVER

INTRODUCTION

Ever since the 4th millennium BC, silver and gold have been highly prized for both decoration and currency. Gold, being soft and malleable with a low melting point, can be easily worked. It was either mined directly from the ground in nuggets or, more usually, extracted in particles by 'panning' with water. A percentage of silver was often found in gold. Called electrum, it was treated as a precious metal in its own right by the ancient Egyptians and Greeks.

Silver, the more common of the two precious metals, has been worked since the 3rd century BC. Silver then came mostly from tin or galena, a lead compound which contained a variable proportion of silver. When the lead was melted off at a low temperature, the silver remained. The practice spread with the Roman Empire from Asia Minor to Europe, particularly to Spain and Hungary. By the 10th century Germany was the main source of silver, but during the 16th century the New World, in particular Mexico and Peru, became Europe's main supplier.

To the ancients gold was associated with the sun, while silver always represented the moon, so much so that silver nitrate is still known as 'lunar caustic'. Gold and pure silver do not tarnish in an unpolluted atmosphere, although silver will discolour in contact with some chlorides and sulphides. For example, egg yolk on a silver spoon will turn it black.

In their purest forms, both gold and silver are too soft for practical use, but the goldsmiths (the term can apply to workers in both silver and gold) of the ancient world overcame the problem by the addition of another metal. Pure gold is termed 24 carat gold. The addition of copper makes the gold reddish in colour, while silver gives it a greenish tinge. White gold contains 25% platinum and is known as 18 carat gold. These precious and therefore expensive metals were open to abuse when alloyed with other cheaper metals. Clearly, some system of regulation was needed. The early assayers adopted the touchstone method whereby gold or silver needles of a known alloy were used to make scratches on a 'touchstone' (any hard, black silicious stone or earthenware), which could then be compared with those on test. Proof of quality, or silver marks, were used in Greece in the 5th century BC, and later the Romans adopted a mark for purity for both gold and silver. In Europe a system of marks for purity, date and place of manufacture was introduced by the French in the 13th century, which came to England after 1300. The 'touch of Paris' for gold and silver was undertaken then, as now, in the hall of the Goldsmiths' Company, hence the name **hallmark**. From 1363 onwards, the maker's name, the place and date of manufacture and the purity were stamped on each piece. An extra mark of the sovereign's head showed that duty payable on weight had been levied. Duty dodgers of the 18th century would have a small piece hallmarked, then cut out the marks and incorporate them into a heavier or larger piece.

THE CRAFT

Two of the earliest methods of fashioning silver, and which are still practised today, were **sinking** and **raising**. The silver ingot was beaten by hammers (or rolled) into a thin sheet and marked with the required shape. This was cut out with shears, and the 'blank' placed on the sinking block – a heavy piece of wood hollowed out in the required shape. The silver sheet was beaten against the inside of the blank with round-headed hammers, row by row, until the entire shape was taken up.

For deeper pieces, such as jugs or bowls, the silversmith worked the silver blank in reverse, by a process called raising. The blank was beaten from the outside over the raising stake, similar to an anvil, a little at a time. A quicker method, practised since the

17th century, was to solder (qv) the sheet into a cone, then raise it into shape.

With both of these methods, when the silver became brittle after constant hammering it was **annealed**. The hammered piece was laid on a special pan or 'hearth' and placed in the flames of a fire. When it was evenly heated through to a dull, red heat, it was plunged into water. The temperature was critical, and gauged solely by an experienced eye from the colour of the piece. The annealing fire was usually in a darkened corner of the workshop, the better to judge the colour.

The piece was finished by **planishing**, which removed the hammer marks and any irregularities in thickness by beating the piece against a smooth surface with a broad, convex-headed hammer.

Another method of making hollow-ware, such as teapots and jugs, was to cut out the sections and **solder** them together. The solder was silver of the same standard, alloyed originally with brass but in modern times with zinc. Great skill was required in soldering so that the joins did not show. Soldering was also used for attaching cast pieces. **Casting** metal, particularly gold and silver, was known to the ancient Chinese who used the 'lost wax' method. The object was modelled in wax and pressed into a mould of sand, then the wax was melted, or 'lost', so leaving the form. The hollow was then filled with molten silver. In England the piece to be cast, such as a spout, handle or foot, was modelled in wood, plaster or metal and placed in a cast of a mixture of sand and clay, known as marl. For very fine work, powdered cuttlefish bone was used to take the impression.

The ancient Egyptians discovered the art of **spinning** sheet-metal. A circular silver sheet was centred on a lathe behind a wooden form in the required shape. As the silver and wood spun together, the turner pressed the silver against the form with a series of tools so that it took on its shape, such as a simple bowl or a baluster-shaped coffee pot. As with raising, the piece had to be annealed throughout. Handles and spouts were soldered on afterwards. It is easy to recognize a spun piece as the concentric rings are clearly visible on the inside – those that were on the outside would have been burnished off in manufacture.

Die-stamping in the 18th century was done by hand. The sheet-silver was hammered into a steel mould to make small objects such as handles for cutlery, buttons and decoration for larger pieces. Following improvements in the 19th century in rolling silver sheets and making hardened steel dies and the water-powered hammer, more and larger pieces could be made. Often candlesticks were stamped out, soldered together and filled for weight.

The finishing of a piece was as important as its manufacture. The discoloration from annealing, the scratches and filemarks were all rubbed off the surface with a compound such as Ayr stone (powdered slate) or pumice. It was then polished with a finer compound of Tripoli stone, red oxide and whiting applied on rotating balls of walrus or buffalo hide. For a highly reflective surface, the piece was **burnished** with a shaped steel or agate tool.

THE DECORATION

There are three main types of decoration for silverware: applied (soldered on), cut (engraved or pierced), and embossed. All three forms might be used on the same piece.

The difference between **chasing** and **embossing** is that with chasing the design is punched out from the front, while with embossing it is worked from behind. The chaser was highly skilled and worked with great precision, making hundreds of punches to give the right texture and style. Very often the chaser decorated a piece from the front after it had been embossed from behind, work known by its French name of *repoussé*. **Flat chasing** was a simpler form of decoration, usually with just an outline punched into the silver. **Engraving** removes the silver with a fine gouge from the surface to form the design, such as a coat of arms. From the 1770s **bright cutting** became fashionable, whereby the edges were polished as the cut was made. **Matting** was another effective decoration, where a series of tiny punch marks were closely and evenly made to give a roughened effect.

Piercing and cut-cardwork were other decorative techniques. With **piercing** the silver was cut right through to make the required design. This might be as simple as the holes in a caster (qv), made with a punch, or a far more elaborate decoration cut with a fine fret-saw, such as an openwork basket. Often, the holed silver was engraved to enhance the effect. With **cut-cardwork**, the design was cut out of a fine sheet of silver and soldered on to the piece. It was widely used by the Huguenots (qv), and consequently came to England in the late 17th century. Leaves and foliate patterns were the most common motifs. Ornamental wires, either stamped with a decorative pattern or swagged, which were hammered into a decorated die, were also used for mounts and decoration.

Gilding, where a thin layer of pure gold was applied to silver, had many uses. It made a silver piece look like gold at a fraction of the cost, it prevented tarnishing, for example on the insides of salt cellars (before they were replaced by blue-glass liners) and it was extremely decorative. When only partially applied it was known as **parcel gilding**. Although the Romans knew that gold could be combined with mercury in an amalgam, it was not until the 17th century that **mercury gilding** was discovered. For this, an amalgam of mercury and gold was painted with a brush on to the silver, which was then fired at a low temperature. The mercury was burnt off, leaving a fine coating of gold. The mercurious oxide gas was highly toxic and was the death of many a mercury gilder from 'the dreaded fossy jaw'. Where there are two or more layers of gold it is known as **double gilding**.

Silver could be applied to a base metal by the same process, but more often other methods were used. **Close-plating** was practised in the 15th century for armour, stirrups and bits, and later used for coating such pieces as knife blades, handles and scissors. The steel was dipped in a bath of sal-ammoniac acid, then into molten tin, and wrapped in silver leaf. Once it had been smoothed down, a hot soldering iron was pressed all over the leaf so that the heat fused the tin to the silver leaf and to the steel. Knife blades were stamped with maker's marks that all too closely resemble hallmarks.

A most ingenious form of plating silver was invented in about 1742 by Thomas Boulsover, a cutler from Sheffield. He discovered a way of uniting copper and silver, when he accidentally overheated the two metals while repairing a knife. His discovery later became known as **Old Sheffield Plate**, named after his city where the industry was later centred. Boulsover's method was to sandwich a copper ingot between two very thin sheets of pure silver. This was bound together with wires and placed in a coke furnace where the metals fused as the silver began to 'weep', at which point the ingot was removed and cooled in water. The solid block was then flattened by power-driven rollers into a thin sheet, which could then be worked in exactly the same way as solid silver. The process was refined in 1760 by Matthew Boulton, who overcame the problem of the exposed edges by soldering silver wire on to them to disguise the copper. Cut-cardwork and punching were clearly not possible with this material as it exposed the copper edges, until a die stamp was invented that 'drew' the silver over the sides. The problem of engraving on to Old Sheffield Plate was overcome in 1790 by substituting the area to be engraved with a thicker-plated piece. By 1810 this had been replaced by the 'rubbed-in shield' method, whereby pure silver was burnished on to the surface of the plate and engraved. These additions can be identified when tarnished, as pure silver and Old Sheffield Plate tarnish at different rates. The introduction in 1830 of a layer of nickel, or German silver, between the copper and silver of the ingot, made it easier to engrave without the copper showing through.

Old Sheffield Plate is sometimes marked (after 1784), sometimes not, so the absence of marks is no clue to age. A crown was used after 1820 to distinguish Old Sheffield Plate from the imported French plate. Sometimes it was marked 'Best Sheffield Heavy Silver Plating' as well. Silver marks were used after 1835.

Old Sheffield Plate was finally overtaken in 1855 by **electroplating**. The process, patented by Henry Wood in 1840, transformed Michael Faraday's laws of electrolysis into a commercial technique. In the same year Wood joined Elkington & Co of Birmingham, who had also been working in that field. The electroplating process that they developed was simple. The piece to be coated, which was usually made of a copper alloy, was immersed on copper wires into a bath of silver potassium cyanide, with an anode of pure silver. A low current was then passed through the anode into the bath for about two hours, by which time a fine coating of silver had transferred from the anode to the article. The major advantage of this method was that when the silver was worn it could be easily replated. The process was inexpensive, and vast quantities of plate were made in the 19th century, particularly domestic pieces for the hotel trade. Anything could be, and was, plated (if covered with a suitable metal powder to react with the anode). With the Victorian passion for naturalism real flowers, ferns, even insects and small animals were electroplated.

THE TYPES

Very few examples of early silverwork have survived. Such was the expense of silver that pieces were often melted down and remodelled when worn out or considered unfashionable. The Dissolution of the Monasteries in the mid-16th centuries not only accounted for much ecclesiastical plate, but also robbed the silversmiths of an important client. However, most of the earliest surviving examples of silver are for non-secular use. Another major loss of plate was to the Royalist cause in the Civil War – Oxford alone yielded up 1,600 lbs of silver from 16 colleges.

DINING TABLEWARE

Until the middle of the 17th century most people ate with their fingers. This necessitated constant washing of the hands before, during and after the meal, in **basins** filled with hot or cold scented water from matching **ewers** brought round by servants. The weight and quality of this plate were indications of wealth. Styles changed with fashion and by the end of the Restoration, when they were no longer in practical use, they became ornate and elaborate. The French late 17th-century helmet style of ewer was typical of the work of the Huguenot goldsmiths.

Since the time of earliest man salt has been a vital preservative and an important flavouring for food. The most important object in plate from the Middle Ages to the 16th century was the **salt** which, as its name implies, held that rare additive. So prized was it that the size and grandeur of the salt was quite out of proportion to the amount it held. The positioning of the 'great salt' or 'salt of estate' on the table was also important. Placing it close to the master showed who was above and, more importantly, who was 'below the salt'.

Salts took on many forms – from architectural, figures, animals (such as the 'Monkey Salt' at New College, Oxford, with an ape holding a crystal bowl on its head), the bell-shaped salts of the 16th century, or a model of the Eddystone Lighthouse dated 1698. Later 17th-century salts were often shaped like an hour glass. Some, called pulley-salts, had three scrolls on top to support a flat dish.

Those dining 'below the salt' from the early 17th century were given their own individual **trencher salts**,

A bell-shaped salt, c.1595

shallow, often triangular or round dishes that were placed beside their trenchers or platters. These were the precursor of the **salt cellar**, the receptacle that has survived to the present day. The shapes of these cellars followed the current fashion. Earlier 18th-century examples are plainer, becoming more fanciful throughout the century – until 1760 they have octagonal bases and a shallow, oval bowl; after 1740 the cauldron-shaped salt standing on three feet or hoofs was in vogue. Oval salts with pierced sides standing on four feet with blue glass liners, and boat-shaped salts, are both typical of the early 19th century. Salt was originally taken with the blade of the knife, but in the early 18th century salt spoons were made for the cellars. Early spoons had shovel-shaped bowls, but they later became cylindrical, with ornate handles such as the whip-thong handle of the 1740s.

The Elizabethan **caster** (or casting bottle) was often a perforated ball holding pepper that formed part of the bell-shaped salt. After the Restoration the pepper caster appeared on the table as one of three or four matching casters for sugar (the largest), ginger, and mustard in a matching pot but without holes in the top. Until the 1760s mustard was sprinkled over the food in dry, powdered form with a **mustard spoon**, the size of a teaspoon but with a longer handle. From then on mustard powder was mixed with milk or water and put in a barrel or tankard-shaped pot, later examples having a blue glass liner.

From the early 18th century these casters were frequently combined with two glass bottles or ewers in a stand called a **cruet**; when it held just two bottles it was called an **oil and vinegar frame** (based on ecclesiastical plate for wine and water). Later versions, all mounted in a single stand, contained any number of cut-glass bottles for oil, soy, mustard, lemon, vinegar, ketchup, pepper and cayenne. **Bottle tickets**, engraved silver plaques that hung round the necks of bottles on chains, identified the contents.

Spice boxes of the mid-18th century generally had two lidded compartments, one for nutmeg, the other for allspice. Between these two was a little silver grater with which to powder the spices on to the food and spiced drinks of the period.

A beautiful but rare piece of table decoration was the **nef**, a finely worked model of a ship with full sails that held the knife and spoon, often the napkin as well. A 'nef salt' was similar in style, but less common.

Another practical piece of table decoration was the **epergne**. In the 18th century the dessert course was eaten either in the dining room after the table had been completely cleared of linen and plate, or in a separate room. The table was laid with puddings, sweetmeats and fruit in an array of glass, porcelain and silver dishes. From the 1720s onwards the epergne stood in the centre of the table and was designed to support a single, shallow, glass bowl and four smaller bowls on arms for all manner of sweetmeats and bonbons. Later designs were highly fanciful, with trees, particularly palm trees, bushes, Chinese pagodas, classical scenes supporting more silver dishes, even candlesticks.

An extravagant, often non-functional object used to decorate the 18th century table was the **centrepiece**. Also known as the *surtout de table*, this extravagant piece took the place of the grand salt. This opportunity to create a great sculpture allowed the rococo and classical silversmith's imaginative and creative skills to run riot. Some incorporated more useful embellishments such as candlebranches, sugar casters and sweetmeat dishes.

The **standing cup**, with a lid but no handles, was a major item of plate in the Middle Ages. It was designed purely as a display of wealth, and not for use, and was a testament to the maker's skill and ingenuity. During the Renaissance rare items were often incorporated into the standing cup, such as an ostrich egg (known as a gryphon's egg), a nautilus shell, or a rare coconut shell that floated ashore from the tropics. The silver standing cup went out of fashion in the 18th century, when it was replaced by a cut-glass version fashioned in similar style.

The term **two-handled cup** describes any cup with two handles, whether purely decorative like a racing cup (a vase with no lid), or practical, usually named

A two-handled silver cup with a cover, c.1735

after the drink it was designed for. A popular drink in the 17th and 18th century was posset, hot milk curdled with wine, vinegar or ale and enriched with spices and served in a **posset pot**. Also common in ceramic, it was bell-shaped and was distinguished by its spout and a lid. It is frequently confused with a **porringer**, a two-handled bowl with a lid designed for soup. A **caudle cup** was for a warm gruel flavoured with wines and spices given to nursing mothers or convalescents. However, these names are thought to be largely Victorian romanticized terms, and whatever cup was to hand was the one that was used. The name porringer is sometimes also given to the **bleeding bowl**, a shallow dish with a handle, supposedly for barbers to bleed their patients in the 17th and 18th centuries. In most cases, this meaning is fanciful, and a skillet cover would be a more accurate description of the piece.

The word **plate** comes from the Spanish *plata* meaning silver, and so describes all wares made of both silver and gold, that is the ornamental gold and silverware exhibited in the eating room, as well as the dinner plates themselves.

Silver (and gold) **dinner plates** were readily used by the rich from Roman times onwards. Few early plates have survived as they became pitted, scratched, scored and cut by knives with constant use. Consequently, these damaged plates were 'boiled, burnished and pickled'. When too bad to resuscitate they were melted down and remade. When fashions changed, for example from plain borders to gadrooned (inverted fluted) borders in 1710, so the plates were remade or remodelled around the edge. Silver was generally used for all the main courses, while gold or gilt plates were used for fruit, which could not tarnish them. Very large oval dishes, called **voiding dishes**, were used to collect the scraps, or 'voided' food, or 'broken meats' from the table.

The process of dining was perfected into an art form by the aristocracy in the 18th century. Dinner lasted many hours, with dozens of different dishes in the two main and two remove courses before the dessert course. Each course was laid out in its entirety, and the food served from the table. Consequently, dinner services had to be very large. Most courses were served on a set of silver **dishes**. Dishes for meat, game and poultry were flat and large for easy carving. A **venison** dish was similar, but with a raised base and gravy well at one end. Fish, and some vegetables, were served in a deeper dish called a **mazarine**, named after Cardinal Mazarin, the late 17th-century French prime minister. This dish had a detachable strainer which fitted tightly over the bowl to drain off any fluid.

The problem of keeping plates and food hot in the dining room was partially overcome in the late 17th century with a **chafing stand**. This small brazier held smouldering charcoal in the bottom and was used for heating food and plates. The later 18th-century stand was a combination of a **dish** or **potato ring** (a pierced silver ring, about 3 inches high, used to keep hot plates and dishes off the table) mounted with a spirit burner. When the chafing stand was combined with a one- or two-handled dish with a lid, it was called a **chafing dish**. A later derivation of the chafing dish, often complete with heater stand, was the **entrée dish** (named in the

A chafing dish

19th century after the course that came between the fish and the joint). This deep dish had a cover with a detachable handle so that it too could be used as a dish. Another ingenious method of keeping sauces warm was with an **Argyle** or Argyll, named after its inventor, the 3rd Duke of Argyll. This late 18th-century warmer resembled a coffee pot in shape, and was fitted with a central tube filled with either hot water or a red-hot metal rod that kept the sauce or gravy warm. Voltaire complained that where the English only had one sauce, they did have several kinds of **sauceboats**. The early 18th-century sauceboat did resemble a boat, with pointed lips at each end and curved handles in the middle. After 1740 the single curved handle was moved to the end, and the bowl supported on feet or a pedestal.

The word **tureen** comes from the French *terrine,* a large earthenware pot for soup or stew. Circular or oval in shape with a lid, the earliest examples date from the 1720s but they were more common later in the century. Their size and shape gave great scope to the silversmith who fashioned them in all styles, from the rich decoration of the rococo to the plainer, classical lines towards the end of the century. After 1760 sets of four, or six, matching **sauce tureens** were an alternative to sauceboats. Matching ladles were a further refinement.

Baskets in silver for bread, cakes and fruit were another challenging medium for the craftsman of the 18th century. They were usually oval in shape, often resembling a wicker basket with plaited silver wire, or cut-work (qv) sides. A feature was the central, swing handle. Smaller versions, with blue glass liners, were for sugar and these often matched the tea canisters (qv).

Food to be served in small dishes was presented on a salver, a flat usually circular tray with a raised rim. The term **waiter** now generally applies to salvers of less than 9 inches diameter, although in the 18th century, when they generally stood on three small feet, it was the accepted term. When the salver has a central, spreading foot it is a dessert stand of a later date. The flat surface of the salver meant that all kinds of decoration were possible, although the most normal was an engraved coat of arms and a highly decorative border.

Many kitchen items were made in silver from the 17th century onwards, more for the amusement of the lady of the house than for the use of the kitchen staff. These included **saucepans** and skillets (with feet), and more unusual pieces like an apple corer, pastry cutter or barding needle (for keeping a slice of bacon in place when larding a game bird or joint of meat). More common from the 17th century were kitchen **peppers** or **spice dredgers**. These silver pieces, modelled on the ordinary kitchen flour dredger, had a cylindrical base with a pierced shallow-domed top. Being of a precious metal, they may have been intended for wig-powder rather than for use in the kitchen. Those with larger holes were **sugar dredgers**, sugar not being as finely ground then as it is today.

One ingenious device made in silver in the late 17th century was the **toasted-cheese dish**, an oblong dish with a reflecting, hinged cover, a wooden handle at the back and a hot water compartment below. Toast, often soaked in wine, was placed on the bottom and cheese (Lancashire was considered the best) was placed on top. The dish was held in front of the fire and the heat was reflected down off the open cover to melt the cheese. Another device was the **griddle**, an 1800 precursor of the barbecue grill. The meat was placed on a silver rack, the ribs being concave in section so that the juices were caught and ran into a broad gutter at the back.

One or two **chamber pots** in silver were usually part of the dining room plate during the 18th and early 19th century until they were superseded by porcelain. In 1575 Queen Elizabeth I ordered 'a round basin and Ewer and piss-pot of silvr. weighg. 57 oz', the earliest recorded silver chamber pot.

CUTLERY

The word cutlery covers all implements with one or more cutting edge, such as swords, daggers, scissors, razors and, of course, domestic knives, although today, the term describes knives, forks and spoons. Whereas knives have been used for eating since man sharpened a flint in the Stone Age, the **fork**, a relatively recent

Silver plate cutlery designed for the future George IV, 1808–12

invention, was introduced into England from Europe in the middle of the 15th century. These forks were used for carving meat rather than for eating, possibly due to the sharpness of the tines. Solid silver forks were known in Italy in the late 14th century, where they were used for eating pasta. The silver tines would not take a sharp point, which may account for their early eating use. The French in the 16th century used a fork to eat food that stained the fingers such as pears and apples cooked in wine, green ginger and candied fruit. Until the mid-17th century the English considered the fork for eating 'foppish', preferring to skewer their food on the point of their knives, or use their fingers.

By the mid-17th century the use of the knife and fork for eating was becoming more common, although King Louis XIV of France, and even Queen Anne as late as the early 18th century, still ate with their fingers. As guests were expected to provide their own cutlery, knives and forks, often spoons as well, were designed as a set and usually cased in a leather pouch .

The handle of the 17th-century **knife** was often very ornate, in ivory, silver, or a hardstone like agate. English blades bore the mark of the Cutlers' Company, a dagger, but the best blades came from Solinghen in Germany, which were exported all over Europe. Until the end of the 17th century the knife blade was pointed, to combine cutting with skewering. In the 18th century silver handles were shaped like a pistol butt, while porcelain and stoneware replaced ivory and agate for both knives and forks. Blades were scimitar-shaped with a blunted end, for eating peas that had become a delicacy; forks, which still had a pair of sharp, straight tines were dangerous for eating, particularly peas.

As with many silver objects, some silver **spoons,** like ceremonial spoons, were designed exclusively for show, but most had a practical use. Until the 17th century it was the custom to give spoons, or sets of spoons, as christening presents. Predictably, the most common styles had religious connections, like the **apostle spoon**, made ideally in sets of 13 (the Master and 12 apostles) but more often found singly. Memorial spoons, engraved with the name or initials of the departed, are of a similar date and style.

Table services of matching cutlery (suitably decorated with the current pattern) came into general use at the turn of the 18th century, when guests were no longer expected to bring their own knives and forks. **Dessert spoons** from the late 18th century differed from table spoons in that they were often gilt. **Basting** or **hash spoons** were larger serving spoons, similar to a kitchen spoon.

ALCOHOLIC DRINKS SILVERWARE

Silver has invariably been connected with drinking, both as a display of wealth and for practical vessels. The Anglo- Saxon **drinking horn** was mounted in silver and supported on silver ball feet. When a tapered bovine horn was cut to make a drinking vessel, it was sealed at the wider end to form a tankard; when sealed at the narrower end, it became a beaker. Until the 18th century, the most common drink for all classes was beer, and for this great numbers of vessels were made. The **tankard** always has a handle and a hinged lid with a thumb piece. The basic tapered, cylindrical shape changed little over the centuries, although the decoration kept pace with the ruling fashion.

Beakers tended to be smaller without handles or

A silver tankard, c.1745

A silver-mounted Gothic wine flagon, c.1851

lids, although there are 'covered' beakers which are decorative. The 'canns' or, as they are better known, **mugs** that appeared in the 1670s hold about half a pint. They are usually cylindrical and always have a handle. The idea of the **tumbler cup** of the late 17th century was that it had sufficient weight in the rounded base to right itself if tipped over. These were also called 'cocking bowls', as they were given as prizes for cockfights. Some came in sets of six and fitted into each other like picnic mugs.

In 1602, one of the *Fifteen directions to Health* advocated by a Dr Vaughan was that 'the cups whereof you drinke should be of silver, or silver and gilt'. The **wine cup**, or goblet, also known as a quaffing cup, appeared at the end of the 16th century. At no more than 8 inches high, it was a smaller version of the standing cup (qv), but without the lid. Despite Dr Vaughan's advice, it was superseded by glass in the mid-18th century.

An open, shallow bowl with a ring handle (something akin to the modern sommelier's taster today) was called a **wine taster** in the mid-17th century. The base was raised to better judge the colour of the wine against the silver. However, although some of these little dishes were undoubtedly made for vintners to sample wine, it is more likely that they were saucers in the true meaning of the word, small dishes for sauce.

The hunting cup of the 18th century was known as a

stirrup cup. Modelled on the 12th century BC Greek *rhyton*, it took the shape of a fox's mask. Other versions in silver had cows', sheep's, boars' or greyhounds' heads. There is even an early 19th-century example of a real fox's mask, mounted in silver with a silver lining to be used as a stirrup cup.

Although beer was the more common drink in the 18th-century dining room, wine was also drunk, particularly by the ladies. The term **wine fountain** is, however, doubly misleading as the object was used to dispense water rather than wine, nor, as it resembled a very grand tea urn with a tap at the bottom, was it a fountain. The water was used for washing the plates between courses in the dining room. The fountain was generally made with a matching **wine cistern** of silver. As with the lead-lined wooden cisterns (qv), this was filled with ice for cooling bottles of wine. It was invariably highly ornate and often very large – the one bought by Catherine the Great of Russia was 5 feet long.

Individual bottle coolers, **wine coolers** or ice pails, date from the early 18th century. Often made in sets of two or four, even six, the neo-classical wine coolers of the late 18th century were modelled on the 5th century BC Greek *kalyx-krater* vases with splayed handles. They were swathed with tell-tale bunches of grapes and other 'Bacchanalian' emblems. Other wine coolers of the same period, inspired by milk pails or banded mahogany cisterns, were obviously simpler.

Bottles did not appear on the table until the end of the 16th century, when they were placed after dinner in a **bottle stand** or **wine coaster** after the servants had left the dining room. Formerly called a **wine slide**, as it 'slid' along the table on a green baize bottom, the 18th-century coaster was circular with either solid or pierced sides of silver (later versions were silver plate) on a turned wooden base. More fanciful coasters of the 19th century ran on wheels, like a cart or gun carriage, and might be joined together in pairs. Some, like the **jolly boat** coaster, were shaped like a rowing boat with twin dishes for the decanters (qv). Whatever their shape, their primary function was to save the table from being scratched.

*A wine label decorated with grapes, vine leaves and
a lion's paw mask, c.1811–12*

Wine labels of the same period were made in every
shape and size, and were hung round the neck of the
decanter or bottle on a chain to identify the wine or
spirit. The decoration was generally symbolic of the
drink – vine leaves and grapes for wine, hops and the
hop leaf for ale, and apples and apple leaves for cider.
Madeira, port, sherry and claret were the most
common labels; gin, though a 'low' drink, was
described as 'Holland'.

Like many continental customs, the fashion for
drinking punch began in England after the Restoration
and continued to the end of the 18th century. Its name
comes from the Hindu word *paunch* meaning 'five',
there being five principal ingredients in punch – a hot
concoction of aqua vitae (usually brandy or, later, rum),
the juice of oranges and lemons, and various spices,
particularly nutmeg and cinnamon. The better **punch
bowls** were of silver, wide, deep bowls on a single foot.
They were often made with a matching **punch ladle**, in
an ornate style such as a stylized shell. The twisted
whalebone handle came in after 1760; smaller versions
are toddy ladles. Often the punch bowl had a detachable
rim so it could double as a monteith. The **monteith** was
similar in shape to a punch bowl, but with a scalloped
rim. It was first recorded by the Oxford antiquarian,
Anthony à Wood, in 1683: 'This yeare in the summer
time came up a vessel or bason notched at the brim to
let drinking glasses hang there by the foot, so that the
body or the drinking place might hang in the water to
cool them. Such a bason was called a "Monteigh", from
a fanciful Scot called "Monsieur Monteigh", who at that

time, or a little before, wore the bottome of his cloake or coate so notched ᴜᴜᴜ '.

Spirits, particularly brandy and rum, were often drunk hot in the 18th century. They were heated in small, ornate saucepans or skillets with wooden handles called **brandy saucepans**.

NON-ALCOHOLIC DRINKS SILVERWARE

Both coffee and tea had been drunk in England before 1660, but with the continental manners and taste introduced after the Restoration, the two beverages became highly fashionable. The diarist John Evelyn mentions coffee in 1637, although it was not until 1652 that a 'Mr Edwards, a Turkey merchant, brought from Smyrna [Ismir] to London one Pasqua Rosee, a Ragusian youth, who prepared this drink for him every morning'. It seems that Mr Edwards tired of his friends dropping in every morning and so allowed his servant ' . . . to sell it publically, and they set up the first coffee house in London . . . The sign was Pasqua Rosee's own head.' The **coffee pot** crafted in silver took on the cylindrical shape of the Eastern coffee pot, with its straight handle mounted halfway down the stem. From then on, the basic conical shape altered little, but the handles, spout and decoration kept pace with the current fashion. In the late 18th century coffee pots matched tea services as they doubled as hot water jugs.

According to the *Publick Advertiser*, chocolate, 'an excellent West Indian drink', was introduced into England in 1657, and was sold alongside coffee. Consequently the **chocolate pot** was similar in shape and style to the coffee pot. However, unlike coffee grounds, chocolate grounds are to be savoured, and to this end the chocolate pot had a movable finial so that a silver stirrer, or molinet, could be inserted and 'swizzled' just before serving. Usually these stirring sticks were fixed permanently to the pot.

Silversmiths and ceramic designers have always worked closely together, the styles adopted by one being followed by the other. A classic example is in the tea service, with teapot, milk jug and sugar basin, that

LEFT *A teapot with stand and lamp, 1705–6*
BELOW *A teapot c.1720*

BELOW *A teapot, c.1800*
RIGHT *A teapot from a tea and coffee set, c.1851*

appeared at the end of the 18th century. Despite its enormous price, tea was extremely popular from the end of the Commonwealth onwards. It was first brewed in Chinese porcelain pots; the first silver **teapot** did not appear until the 1670s. This early teapot resembled the coffee pot of the same date, but by 1685 it had become more rounded, modelled on a Chinese wine pot with a spout that is similar to the shape of the present day teapot. Again like the coffee pot, the general proportions of the teapot remained constant, but the shape, style and decoration altered with the current fashion. Until the mid-17th century, teapots were either pear-shaped, generally on a stand, or globular. By 1740 the inverted pear shape was the fashion that lasted until the mid-1770s, when silver teapots became less desirable than porcelain ones.

After 1770 the reduction in the price of tea meant that it was widely drunk and all manner and shapes of teapots were made. In the 1780s and 90s the prevailing shape was a plain oval, although the designers of the day, like Adam (qv), produced designs for teapots in the current neo-classical style. Tea services became popular during the Regency. Throughout the 19th century no one shape predominated. Very small versions of teapots made between 1725 and 1775 were for saffron tea, taken for medicinal purposes.

It is surprising that, for a commodity as valuable as sugar was in the 17th century, there are no sugar bowls from this period. The earliest container, the **sugar box**, appeared in the 1670s and was round and squat with a lid. From then on they took many forms. Later **sugar bowls** and **basins** were also circular, often with a cover, and these developed into the **sugar vases** of the mid-18th century. Sugar cane was supplied in 'loaf' form (usually shaped like a cone) and was cut up with **crushers**. The silver version, a flimsy, flat circular disc from the early 19th century, coincided with the advent of softer sugar made from sugar beet. **Sugar nippers**, like toy fire tongs, date from the 1690s, but were supplanted by **tongs** in the 1760s.

Although the Chinese drank warm milk with their tea, the practice did not take hold in England until the early 18th century, when 'milk potts' were made. Cream was drunk in tea towards the end of the century, and these cream jugs were objects of great fancy and style – some from the 1760s were shaped like a cow, others had goats' heads. They are characterized by a wide lip, to make pouring of thick cream easier, hence the popularity of the helmet style in the mid-18th century. The silver **tea cup and saucer** had little life beyond the Restoration, when everything was tried in silver.

The **tea kettle and stand**, like a teapot with a little spirit burner below, was introduced in the late 17th century to heat the water for making the tea. The burner stood on a little tripod with wooden feet to protect the table from the heat; in rare cases, the tripod table was also of silver in the same style. Due to the

A kettle from a Gothic tea and coffee set

difficulties of finding a suitable fluid for the burner (spirit of wine was effective but very expensive), tea kettles were superseded by the tea urn.

The **tea** (or coffee) **urn** had the same purpose as the tea kettle. The first tea urns, with a spigot tap below, appeared in about 1760. The water was heated by a little charcoal burner below. Later models, mostly of Old Sheffield Plate, had a central tube in which fitted a red-hot cast iron bar to heat the water. With this method of heating, the urn could have a more elegant design. Nevertheless, by the end of the century the spirit lamp had returned.

Such was the price of tea that it was kept locked in a silver box known as a **canister**. Often two or three, sometimes even more, matching canisters were made to hold different kinds of tea. Later these were called **tea caddies** (qv). By the end of the 18th century almost every shape imaginable was employed for the tea caddy, although neo-classical designs such as Grecian urns predominated. Until the 1740s the cup-shaped lid of the canister doubled as a measure for the tea; thereafter a series of ladles or **caddy spoons,** made with their stems almost vertical to the bowl, became fashionable. These were often rather fanciful, with representations of leaves, shells, jockey-caps, fish, even mandarins.

LIGHTING SILVERWARE

Very few silver **candlesticks** have survived from much before the 17th century, but those that have tend to be short with a wide drip pan near the bell-shaped base. The overhanging drip pan was to protect the hand when carrying the candlestick. By the 1680s candlesticks were being cast, giving reign to greater decoration on a basic Doric column shape. The foot was large, square, octagonal or circular in shape, often two thirds of the height in width to give greater stability. From then on the shape of silver candlesticks generally followed those of brass (qv). However, being of a more costly medium, silver candlesticks tended to have more embellishment, particularly those in the rococo style. Candlesticks of the neo-classical period were plainer, such as the simple reeded columns with Corinthian capitals on a square base decorated with swags, wreaths and draperies. The plainer version still had a round or elliptical base, with either an urn in the pedestal stem under the socket, or an inverted bell for the socket.

Until the introduction of the oil lamp candles were a major source of light, and therefore two or more branches with sockets were fitted to the tops of a single candlestick, to form a **candelabrum**. Single candlesticks and candelabra were made in sets to stand on a long table and around the room, often forming part of a complete dinner service. With the advent of Old Sheffield Plate, candelabra could be very elaborate. Frequently the arms were made in Old Sheffield Plate, while the base was of solid silver. In some cases the branches were a later addition.

Bed-chamber or **hand candlesticks** were designed to be carried, hence the wide, circular drip pan base and handle. When combined with snuffer scissors and extinguisher (qv), it was more likely to have been used by a servant tending the candles in the house than merely for lighting the way to bed.

In an account of the French ambassador's visit to Hampton Court in 1527 it is recorded that 'the plates that hung on the walls to give light in the chamber

*A silver-gilt
candelabrum with
Grecian design motifs,
c.1815*

were of silver and gilt, with lights burning in them'.
The idea of the **wall sconce** was to reflect the light from
a single or double candle off the highly polished surface
out into the room. From the Restoration onwards they
were generally oval in shape, surrounded by scrolled
decoration. Later examples had a mirrored glass panel
for the same purpose. The fashion lasted until the
beginning of the 18th century.

Vital to the efficient burning of candles were silver
snuffer scissors, for trimming or extinguishing the
wick. As the scissors cut the wick, the cutting blade
fitted neatly into a small box, so trapping the
extinguished wick. The scissors were either placed on a
silver pan or tray, or rested on their own stand.
Snuffers, or podia, were usually conical in shape and
often mounted on a long pole for high candles.

WRITING SILVERWARE

The **taper-stick**, a miniature candlestick, dates from the
late 17th century when correspondence was becoming a
major pastime. The flame was used to melt the wax for
sealing letters, and consequently taper-sticks were often

made in conjunction with **inkwells**. The **taper-stand** or **wax-jack** served an identical purpose, save that the candle was a long turpentine-waxed taper that was wound on a reel and fed through a nozzle. Later 18th-century versions had the coil inside a drum, one ingeniously operating the coiled taper mechanically.

Although the word was in use in the 15th century, there are no known surviving examples of a **standish** from before 1625. The silver **Treasury** standish had three compartments, for ink, sand or 'pounce', and wafers. The ink was contained in a ceramic (sometimes horn) pot, later in glass inkwells. The pounce was powdered sandarac, the gum from the thuja or 'gum sandarac tree' from North Africa, which was sprinkled over the parchment to make it take the ink, or rubbed into writing paper to make it less absorbent for the ink. The sand was sprinkled over the paper to dry the wet ink. The wafer was not the blotting paper but a small disc of flour mixed with gum or gelatine and a colouring agent which, when moistened, was used for sealing letters. Like sealing wax which was also commonly used, it took an impression from a seal. Below was a tray that held the dip pens. Other variations included little silver pots filled with shot to clean the nib of the pen. Some incorporated taper-sticks or wax-jacks. Such was the irregularity of the post, it was often necessary to summon a servant the moment a letter was written. Small hand bells formed part of the standish, often doubling as covers for one of the pots. As pen-knives (protected blades for cutting and shaping quill pens) were so essential to writing, it is surprising that they did not form part of the standish.

Goose or duck quill pens, dipped in ink, were the only form of writing implement until the late 17th century, when a rudimentary form of silver fountain pen was invented – Pepys had 'a pen with a resevoir' which he bought for £5. These pens, simple tubes with detachable quill nibs, were included on silversmiths' trade cards throughout the 18th century, while George IV owned a patent 'penograph or writing instrument' in 1826 that held enough ink for up to 12 hours' writing.

BEDROOM SILVERWARE

One of the many fine pieces and ideas to filter through from the Continent after the Restoration was the **toilet set**. Occasionally in silver, but more usually in silver-gilt, it was traditionally the wedding gift from husband to wife – Charles II gave one costing £4,000 to his queen. The many separate items fitted neatly into a box for travelling. According to the eloquent John Evelyn, it comprised:

> Of Toilet Plate Gilt, and Embossed,
> And several other things of Cost,
> The Table Mirror, one Glue Pot,
> One for Pomatum, and what not?
> Of Washes, Ungents, Cosmetiks,
> A pair of Silver Candlesticks,
> Snuffers and Snuff Dish, Boxes more
> For Powders, Patches, Water Store,
> In Silver Flasks or Bottles, Cups
> Covered or open to wash chaps.

These pieces described by Evelyn were just the basics. Pomatum was an apple lotion 'which is of use to soften and supple the roughness of the skin', which was put into a **chap bowl** or just used for water, as mentioned

A silver scent bottle, 1546

173

by Evelyn. The boxes held patches (hence the glue in the glue pot) for the pock-marked face, and powder for the face and hair. These toilet sets often included ewers and basins for washing, large boxes, called comb boxes, hairbrushes (even beard brushes), clothes brushes called **whisks,** and combs. There was always a box with a pin-cushion lid, often a pin tray as well. Also part of the toilet set was a pair of 'dressing weights' or 'plummits', twin bottles with hooks on the caps to hang them from, thought to be for keeping dressing-table covers in place.

Other silver pieces connected with the late 18th-century toilet are **toothbrushes,** with detachable ivory and bristle heads that fitted in a silver case, a **toothe-powder** box and a **tongue-scraper,** a narrow, springy bow of silver with an ivory finial at each end to 'attend to the furry tongue'.

'A Shaving basyn of sylver and a ewer' are recorded in an inventory dated 1521. These **shaving basins** were common throughout the ages. The shaving dish was generally oval in shape with a semicircle shape cut out of the middle to fit around the neck of the person being shaved. **Shaving sets** included razors, a spherical **soap ball box,** a shaving brush and various boxes for lotions. A cased shaving set was known as a **dressing case** – some in the late 18th century were fitted with an ingenious travelling shaving bowl with a stand and heater.

And the ultimate silver object – a nipple shield. This pierced shield, about an inch in diameter, encased the nursing mother's nipple. It was designed supposedly to 'prevent breast milk from soiling clothes'. After all, it was a short step for one born with a silver spoon in their mouth to feeding from a silver nipple.

TEXTILES

INTRODUCTION

The term 'textiles' describes the whole science of woven fabric that includes silks, velvets and tapestry. 'Embroidery' is the decoration of the basic fabric.

THE TYPES

EMBROIDERY

Because of its extreme fragility few examples of early embroidery have survived, although a few fragments from the 4th and 3rd centuries BC have been found in the Crimea and some Roman pieces in Egypt from the 2nd century AD. The English excelled in ecclesiastical embroidery in the mid-13th and 14th centuries. **Opus Anglicanum**, or 'English work', was greatly respected all over Europe and ordered in large quantities. Although much of this work survives, most secular work of the same period has perished. The skills declined after 1350, but were revived towards the end of the 16th century.

Elizabethan embroidery, mostly executed by the aristocracy, was famed for its design and execution – Queen Elizabeth I herself and her Court were all accomplished needlewomen, as was Mary, Queen of Scots, who, with Bess of Hardwicke, worked the Oxborough Hangings, a series of panels depicting exotic animals and flowers. It was the main occupation of the châtelaine, the female members of her family, and servants, who were all tutored by professional embroiderers who travelled from house to house teaching them the skills of needlework. The practice of employing a resident teacher continued to the 18th century. Elizabethan portraits show richly embroidered clothes, dresses and chemises, shirts and sleeves, in coloured silks, more often in **blackwork** where the curling design was worked in black silk on white linen.

When gold or silver thread was incorporated into the piece, it was known as **couching**; often the design or motif was filled in with more blackwork.

Although a carpet-knot was used when working wool on hemp or linen for **Turkey work**, or set work, it is still classed as embroidery. The technique was developed by English carpet weavers during the 16th century, who copied the rich pile and designs of Turkish carpets. With this somewhat geometrical approach to mainly floral subjects, it was very popular in the 17th century for cushions, chair backs and seats. Later, weavers discovered how to knot the pile during the weaving process, to similar effect.

Another decorative covering for chairs and sofas was worked in needlepoint, again often by the ladies of the house. They used a variety of stitches on plain canvas:

A design for embroidery, early 17th century

Blackwork

Crewel work

176

gros-point (so similar in look to tapestry that it was often erroneously called tapestry work) and the finer stitch, **petit-point** or **tent stitch**.

Raised embroidery, where some of the ornament was padded to give a three-dimensional effect known as **stump work**, was fashionable from about 1625 to the end of the century. It was used to cover jewel boxes, mirror surrounds, book spines and picture frames in a rich miscellany of designs, usually animals, figures (often Old Testament themes), plants and insects all wonderfully out of scale. The faces and limbs of the figures were carved wood or covered with silk and painted. Stump work reached the height of its popularity during the Restoration. When a leopard is portrayed, it is in honour of Charles II's wife, Catherine of Braganza, the leopard being the emblem of Braganza.

Another form of embroidery used from the mid-16th century onwards for wall and bed-hangings, and for curtains, was known as **crewel work** or 'Jacobean embroidery'. It was a highly decorative medium, where cotton twill or linen was embroidered with wools either in bright colours or in various shades of green. The tree of life with its waving stem covered with a mass of chintz flowers, set on a stylized hillock, was a common design. Other patterns were copied from 'palampored', printed Indian cotton. Crewel work continued into the 18th century and, like the furniture it often adorned, it became lighter and more delicate.

The early **samplers** (the generic name for any small piece of embroidery) of the 17th century were designed to show the variety of stitches. They were generally worked on loosely woven linen with coloured threads, sometimes gold and silver as well, depicting a whole bestiary of animals and herbs. By the 18th century samplers had become an exercise for beginners, particularly young girls. These are generally square and decorated with the alphabet, a religious text, a few flowers, the name and age of the child and the date it was worked. The vogue for making **map samplers**, where the outline was 'drawn' in black silk, began around 1770 and lasted until the 1840s.

During the 18th century the fashion for clothes of muslin prompted all manner of needlework decoration.

Collectively known as **whitework**, the designs and stitches employed by women to decorate their clothes and linen were very fine and imaginative. The **Dresden** or **pulled work** used various 'pull' stitches on fine muslin to draw it into patterns, so leaving open areas to create the impression of lace. The rest of the design was worked with a fine surface stitch. It was much used for ruffles, cuffs, kerchiefs and other delicate accessories. Later, it was combined with **tambour work**, a form of chain stitch worked with a steel hook on material stretched over a frame like a tambourine.

Ayrshire work, named after the Scottish county where it originated, became fashionable in the late 18th century. Areas of muslin were cut away and the edges oversewn. Also known as **broderie anglaise**, it remained popular for christening robes, underwear and sleeve frills well into the 19th century. A refinement was to fill the 'hole' with lace.

A wide variety of stitches and subjects have been used for **embroidered pictures** since the mid-17th century. The early pictures formed part of a larger decoration, like a valance, bed-hanging or cushion, and frequently depicted Old Testament scenes and allegorical subjects such as the Virtues. The work was extremely fine, the faces sewn in a 'split stitch', where the single silk thread actually 'splits' each stitch to give an effect of shading. By the mid-18th century paintings and engravings were copied on to canvas and worked over in fine coloured or black silks, and occasionally horse hair, even human hair. Often the faces and hands were painted in watercolour. **Mourning pictures**, where members of the family are depicted around the departed's tomb, were a typical use of this medium.

Pictures and decorations of the 19th century were created in **plush work** and **chenille work**. Plush work stands proud of the canvas and is created by looping the thread to the required height and then cutting the loops. Chenille work is also raised, but is made with a thick silk, or silk and wool, thread that is 'furry', like a *chenille*, a caterpillar in French.

Although it had been in existence since 1810, it was not until the 1830s with the rise of the leisured middle class that **Berlin wool work** really became fashionable. The wools, often bright and garish in colour, were imported from Berlin together with the design printed on squared paper. This design was then worked in cross stitch, or gros-point, by translating the stitches on the paper on to the canvas by counting – a simple process, even for the most unskilled. Nothing escaped this medium, from chair covers, carpets and bell-pulls, to waistcoats, slippers and pictures. Pictures of ships, where hull and rigging are correct in every detail, are usually the work of sailors.

Beads, pearls and precious stones, even pieces of mirrored glass, have been applied to fabric for centuries, but the passion for **beadwork**, where the decoration is made up in coloured beads sewn to the canvas, belongs to the Victorians. It was widely used for the decoration of cushions and stools, and other small pieces such as pin cushions, spectacle cases and slippers.

Applied work or appliqué is another early method of decoration that evolved over the centuries. In its simplest form, the design was cut out from one piece of cloth and secured and outlined by embroidery on another. In the Middle Ages it was widely used as a cheaper substitute for tapestry. In the 16th and 17th century, appliqué was used for all decorative work, from chair covers to horse-trappings: the richest works were velvet cushions and hangings appliquéd with satin. Where the appliquéd patch was incorporated into the cloth, it was known as **counterpoint**.

On similar lines to appliqué, **quilting** was widely used by the rich during the 17th and 18th centuries. It was made by stitching two pieces of material together with a layer of wool or flock in between. The design was then formed by stitching on top. In the early 1600s quilted doublets and breeches were quite the fashion; quilted bedspreads and bolster-cases were the most common uses, some with additional embroidery or appliqué. In the 18th century quilted satin petticoats, nightcaps and dressing gowns were essential garments against the cold in winter. Where the design 'wiggles' around, it is called **vermicule**, after the French for worm. **Italian quilting** (Italian by name, but not by origin) had two lines of parallel stitching, threaded with a cord, to form the pattern to give it a raised effect.

The art of making candlewick bedspreads came from America. The design, usually some patriotic emblem or flowers and fruit, was embroidered with the same thick cord as the wick of a candle.

TAPESTRY

Tapestry is a woven fabric where the design is formed by the coloured weft (lateral) threads being woven into the warp (longitudinal). The technique of weaving tapestries was known to the ancient Egyptians, Greeks and Romans. The earliest tapestries in Europe were made at the turn of the 14th century, when they were called **Arras** tapestries after the French town of their manufacture. The name 'arras' for tapestry, often used by Shakespeare and the diarist John Evelyn, became obsolete at the end of the 17th century.

William Sheldon, a Warwickshire squire of the late 16th century, was the patron of the factory that made the earliest English tapestries, known as **Sheldon** tapestries. Production continued after his death, under his son and grandson. The best known Sheldon tapestries are maps of Warwickshire and neighbouring counties.

In 1619 Sir Francis Crane, under the patronage of James I, founded a tapestry manufactuary at **Mortlake** in Surrey, and Flemish weavers were smuggled out of their own country to staff it. Consequently, the tapestries it produced were Flemish in character and mostly of Biblical or classical scenes. The fame of the fine Mortlake tapestries spread, but unfortunately for Crane much of the factory's work was for Charles I who was slow to pay, or declined. Eventually, Crane's brother, who inherited the factory in 1636, sold it to the king and it became known as the King's Works. Mortlake continued production during the Commonwealth and the Restoration, closing at the end of the century, by which time **Soho**, Fulham and Lambeth had replaced Mortlake as weaving centres. William Morris revived the medieval art of weaving tapestries at **Merton Abbey** in the late 19th century, but his factory closed in the 1920s.

HOUSES OPEN TO THE PUBLIC

The houses listed below are just a few open to the public where some of the items mentioned in the text can be seen. Those marked * belong to the National Trust.

Avon:
*Clevedon Court, Clevedon (0275 872257)
17th/19th-century furniture, ceramics, Nailsea glass

*Dyrham Park, nr Chippenham (0272 372501)
18th-century furniture, state bed, ceramics (especially delftware), tapestries and furnishing textiles

Bedfordshire:
Luton Hoo, Luton (0582 22955)
furniture, Ludlow collection of English porcelain and maiolica, tapestries

Woburn Abbey (0525 290666)
English and French furniture, ceramics, glass, Huguenot silver and tapestries

Berkshire:
*Basildon Park, Lower Basildon, Reading (0734 843040)
18th-century furniture, including fine state bed

Buckinghamshire:
*Ascott, Wing, Leighton Buzzard (0296 688242)
18th-century furniture including Chinese lacquer, Chinese porcelain

Chicheley Hall, Newport Pagnell (023065 252)
18th- and 19th-century furniture

Cambridgeshire:
*Angelsey Abbey, Lode (0223 811200)
furniture, porcelain, silver and tapestries

Elton Hall, Peterborough (0832 280468)
17th/19th-century furniture

Cheshire:
*Dunham Massey, Altrincham (061 9411025)
18th-century walnut furniture, Huguenot silver

*Little Moreton Hall, Congleton (0262 272018)
early furniture including good example of long table, pewter

*Lyme Park, Disley, Stockport (0663 762023)
18th-century furniture, Mortlake tapestries

*Tatton Park, Knutsford (0565 654822)
18th- and 19th-century (Regency) furniture, silver and glass

Cornwall:
*Antony House, Torpoint (0752 812191)
early 18th-century furniture, important 18th- and 19th-century ceramics, later tapestries

181

*Cotehele, St Dominick, nr Saltash (0579 50434)
16th- and 17th-century oak furniture, tapestries and early furnishing textiles

*Lanhydrock, Bodmin (0208 73320)
complete example of Victorian house

Pencarrow, Bodmin (020884 369)
17th/19th-century furniture (including Chinese cabinets), 18th- and 19th-century porcelain including Worcester and Spode, glass, bedspreads, Jacobean crewel work, Berlin work and gros-point sofas and chairs

Prideau Place, Padstow (0841 532945)
17th/19th-century furniture, ceramics, glass including Bristol Blue

*St Michael's Mount, Marazion, nr Penzance (0736 710507)
17th- and 18th-century furniture, English silver

Cumbria:
Dalemain, nr Penrith (07684 86450)
English 17th/19th-century furniture, 18th-century blue-and-white Chinese export porcelain, glasses

Muncaster Castle, Ravenglass (0229 717614)
furniture, ceramics (including important Derby dinner service), silver (some by Paul Storr), tapestries and needlework panels

Derbyshire:
*Calke Abbey, Ticknall (0332 863822)
17th/19th-century furniture including baroque state bed

Chatsworth, Bakewell (0246 582204)
English 17th- and 18th-century furniture, porcelain, glass and tapestries

*Hardwick Hall, Doe Lea, Chesterfield (0246 850430)
16th/19th-century furniture, important embroideries and tapestries

*Kedleston Hall, Derby (0332 842191)
18th-century furniture by Adam

Devon:
*Knightshayes Court, Bolham, Tiverton (0884 254665)
collection of 17th-century maiolica

*Saltram, Plymouth (0752 336546)
18th-century furniture including carved giltwood suite possibly by Chippendale, tapestries

Dorset:
*Kingston Lacey, Wimborne Minster (020 883402)
18th- and 19th-century furniture, tapestry and furnishing textiles

Gloucestershire:
Berkley Castle, Berkley (0453 810332)
17th/19th-century English and Chinese furniture, Mortlake tapestries and petit-point

Stanway House, Cheltenham (038673 469)
English 17th- and 18th-century furniture, ceramics including Chelsea Red Anchor period

Sudeley Castle, Winchcombe (0242 602308)
17th/19th-century furniture, porcelain, needlework and tapestries

Hampshire:
*The Vyne, Sherborne St John, Basingstoke (0256 881337) 17th- and 18th-century furniture, Soho tapestries

Hereford and Worcester:
Eastnor, Ledbury (0531 633160) 17th/19th-century furniture, needlework and 17th- and 18th-century tapestries

Hertfordshire:
Hatfield House, Hatfield (0707 262823) 17th/19th-century furniture, needlework and tapestries

Kent:
*Knole, Sevenoaks (0732 450608) 17th-century state furniture including the 'King's bed' and silver furniture, fine porcelain and textiles

Leeds Castle, Maidstone (0622 765400) medieval, 17th/19th-century furniture, ceramics, silver, tapestries from 15th century

Squerryes Court, Westerham (0959 562345) 17th- and 18th-century furniture, ceramics, needlework and Soho tapestries

Lancashire:
Hoghton Tower, nr Preston (025 485 2986) 17th/19th-century furniture, collection of ceramic teapots

Lincolnshire:
*Belton House, Grantham (0476 66116) 18th-century furniture, ceramics, English display and table silver, tapestries

Belvoir Castle, Grantham (0476 870262) 17th/19th-century furniture, glass, tapestries

Burghley House, Stamford (0780 52451) 17th- and 18th-century English furniture, Chinese porcelain, glass, tapestries

Middlesex:
*Osterley Park, Isleworth, Middlesex (081 560 3918) collection of furniture by Adam, tapestries

Syon Park, Brentford (081 560 0881) 18th-century furniture

Norfolk:
*Blickling Hall, Aylsham (0263 733084) 18th-century furniture, tapestries and furnishing textiles

Holkham Hall, Wells-next-the-Sea (0328 710227) 18th- and 19th-century furniture, tapestries

*Oxburgh Hall, nr King's Lynn (036 621258) 17th/19th-century furniture, 16th-century tapestries

Northamptonshire:
Althorp, Althorp, Northampton (0604 770006) 17th- and 18th-century furniture, rare English porcelain

Boughton House, Kettering (0536 515731) 17th- and 18th-century furniture, porcelain

*Canons Ashby, Daventry (0327 860044) 18th-century furniture, pewter, English collection of 17th- and 18th-century tapestries

Rockingham Castle, Market Harborough (0536 770240) 17th- and 18th-century furniture, ceramics (collection of Rockingham)

Northumberland:
Alnwick, Alnwick (0665 510777) 17th/19th-century furniture, ceramics (including Chelsea), silk wall covers and tapestries

*Wallington, Cambo, Morpeth (067074 283) 18th- and 19th-century furniture (including pieces by Chippendale and Sheraton), 18th-century soft-paste porcelain (rare Bow figures), needlework panels

Oxfordshire:
Blenheim Palace, Woodstock (0993 811091) 18th- and 19th-century furniture, ceramics, tapestries

*Buscot Park, Faringdon (0367 242094 not weekends) Regency and empire furniture, Oriental porcelain

Shropshire:
*Attingham Park, Shrewsbury (074377 203) Grand Tour collection, furniture from Gillow's of Lancaster, Regency silver

*Benthall Hall, Broseley, Telford (0952 882159) 17th- and 18th-century furniture, Welsh pewter, porcelain

Weston Park, Weston-under-Lizard (095276 201) 18th-century furniture

Staffordshire:
Shugborough, nr Stafford (0889 881388) 18th-century English chinoiserie furniture, collection of 18th-century ceramics (including Chinese export armorial dinner service), Irish cut-glass chandelier, 18th- and 19th-century textiles and tapestries

Suffolk:
*Ickworth, Bury St Edmunds (0284 735270) 18th-century furniture, 17th- and 18th-century silver

Somerleyton Hall, Lowestoft (0502 730224) 18th- and 19th-century furniture, ceramics (including collection of Lowestoft), glass, tapestries

Surrey:
*Clandon Park, West Clandon (0483 222482) 18th-century furniture, 17th- and 18th-century porcelain and Mortlake tapestries

*Ham House, Richmond (081 940 1950) 17th-century furniture

*Polesdon Lacey, nr Dorking (0372 458203) 18th-century furniture, ceramics

Sussex:
Arundel Castle, Arundel (0903 883136) 15th/19th-century furniture, needlework and tapestries

Firle Place, nr Lewes (0273 858335) 17th/19th-century English furniture, ceramics

*Petworth House, (0798 42207)
17th/19th-century furniture
(including rococo pier glasses
and tables)

Warwickshire:
Arbury Hall, Nuneaton
(0203 382804)
17th- and 18th-century
furniture, ceramics, glass,
needlework

Coughton Court, Alcester
(0789 400777)
ceramics (including Worcester
dessert service, also Coalport
service), needlework and
tapestries

Ragley Hall, Alcester
(0789 762090)
18th-century English furniture,
18th-century ceramic collection

West Midlands:
*Baddesley Clinton, Knowle,
Solihull (0564 783294)
17th- and 18th-century oak
furniture

Hagley Hall, Stourbridge
(0562 882408)
18th-century furniture,
tapestries by Mortlake and
Joshua Morris

*Moseley Old Hall, Fordhouses,
Wolverhampton (0902 782808)
17th-century oak furniture,
delftware

Wiltshire:
*Mompesson House, The Close,
Salisbury (0722 335659)
18th- and 19th-century
furniture, porcelain and
18th-century drinking glasses

*Stourhead, Stourton,
Warminster (0747 840348)
18th-century furniture

(including some by the younger
Chippendale)

Worcestershire:
*Hanbury Hall, Droitwich
(0527 821214)
18th- and 19th-century
furniture, Chelsea, Derby and
Bow figures

Longleat House, Warminster
(0985 844400)
17th/19th-century furniture,
glass, tapestries

Yorkshire:
*Beningbrough Hall,
Shipton-by-Beningbrough, York
(0904 470666)
17th- and 18th-century
furniture including important
walnut furniture, baroque state
bed with hangings, Oriental
blue-and-white and *famille
verte*

Castle Howard, York
(0653 384444)
18th- and 19th-century
furniture, ceramics, decorative
glass, tapestries

*East Riddlesden Hall, Keighley
(0535 607075)
17th/19th-century oak furniture
including early press cupboard,
pewter, 17th-century
needlework

Fairfax House, York
(0904 655543)
18th-century English furniture,
Chinese porcelain, glass

*Nostell Priory, Nostell, nr
Wakefield (0924 863892)
18th- and 19th-century
furniture, including important
pieces made by Chippendale,
tapestries

SCOTLAND
Berwickshire:
Paxton House,
Berwick-upon-Tweed
(0289 86291)
18th-century furniture
including important collection
made for the house by Thomas
Chippendale

Edinburgh:
Hopetoun House, South
Queensferry (031 3312451)
English and Scottish 17th- and
18th-century furniture,
ceramics, original 18th-century
wall damask

Peebleshire:
Traquair House, Innerleithen
(0896 830023)
17th- and 18th-century
furniture, ceramics, glass,
needlework, tapestries

Perthshire:
Scone Palace, Perth
(0738 52300)
18th-century furniture,
ceramics, needlework

Roxboroughshire:
Floors Castle, Kelso
(0573 223333)
English and Scottish
18th-century furniture,
ceramics, tapestries

Selkirk:
Bowhill, Selkirk (0750 20732)
English 17th/19th-century
furniture, ceramics, decorative
glass, tapestries

Sutherland:
Dunrobin Castle, Golspie
(0408 633177)
English 18th-century furniture,
collection of Wemyss ware,
Mortlake tapestries

WALES
Clwyd:
*Chirk Castle (0691 777701)
English furniture, pewter,
Mortlake tapestries

*Erddig, Wrexham
(0978 355314)
18th- and early 19th-century
furniture (including gilt pier
glasses and girandoles), Chelsea
and Worcester porcelain,
delftware

Powys:
*Powis Castle, Welshpool
(0938 554336)
19th-century furniture, early
tapestries

NORTHERN IRELAND
Co. Fermanagh:
*Florence Court, nr Enniskillen
(036 582249)
18th-century Irish furniture,
Aubusson carpets, Waterford
glass

Co. Tyrone:
The Argory, Moy, Dungannon
(08687 84753)
18th- and 19th-century
furniture (including
mosaic-topped tables from the
Grand Tour), gas lights

INDEX

187